Cricket at the grassroots

Humorous memories of
the Sussex club game

by
Dick Redbourn

ISBN 1 85770 095 3

Printed at The Authors' Publishing Guild,
Hadlow Down, East Sussex
01825 830319

Copies of this book, price £10.50 (including p&p) are available from:
S.B. Publications, 19 Grove Road, Seaford. E.Sussex BN25 1TP.
or
Dick Redbourn, 12 Harecombe Rise, Crowborough, E.Sussex TN6 1LX

'With thanks to the greatest game, for the best fun part of my life'

ACKNOWLEDGEMENTS

To all my cricketing friends and acquaintances, who've allowed me to 'bash their ears' for information while writing this book. The details, anecdotes and above all, stories I've gleaned, have been invaluable in fleshing out my memories, and providing new material.

Special thanks to Steve Collins, whose superb, highly professional, graphic design work, is responsible for the book's layout and visual appeal.

and to Ron Baker, for his delightful caricature of Puttie.

and to Maureen and Adrian.

Front cover photograph:
Classic mid-'70's shot of Tony DaVall's crumpled, buckskin boots, not long before their demise. Details of their origins are lost in the mists of antiquity.

Back cover photograph:
St. James's Montefiore C.C. Ground at Ditchling in 1995.

By the same author: The Domestic Cricketer
Midas Books (1977)

CONTENTS

BY MICHAEL JAYSTON

This book should be a very welcome addition to the library of every cricket lover, especially when there are so few books written about the richness of the game at amateur club level.

I am particularly pleased to write the foreword because I know, or have heard of, most of the characters of whom Dick Redbourn writes with such affection. The book abounds with hilarious incidents, one in particular concerning Tony Salisbury, having matches arranged for him until the end of October, so he could complete his thousand runs for the season.

There is a wonderful politically incorrect chapter entitled, 'Our long-suffering women', which makes me wonder how on earth we men managed to get away with the cavalier treatment of our ladies: marriages postponed until the season was over; wives in labour while their partners were playing in a 'vital' match. Most of Dick's stories are 'pre-breatherlyser'. Any team travelling to away games nowadays comprises at least three disgruntled players who are designated to drive the others, sometimes drawing lots for the dubious privilege. It's surprising that in Dick's day, considering the copious amounts of beer consumed, that there were so few accidents. Perhaps the police in those days were not on the look out for cars proceeding at 15 mph.

It is interesting to note that the majority of anecdotes in this book hardly ever involve League cricket. There must be some psychological reason for this. Friendly games seem to inspire more eccentricity. Some League games are matches of attrition, wearing down the opposition, and with little humour and often a good deal of boredom. Non-League matches in many cases are much more of a challenge, risks taken, the gauntlet thrown down and accepted, flamboyant batting. Games between teams who have been rivals for years can also be far more competitive than playing a League match for a piddling batting or bowling point.

Heroes and eccentrics shine out of this book; the great local batsman Gerry Jarman – one hundred centuries at club level, his record for the aggregate runs in a season for Rottingdean (1,741) standing for twenty years. Noel Bennett enters the list of eccentrics when for years he organised matches played on Christmas Day! Now there's glorious madness for you.

As with all books written about cricket this is primarily a book about humour, the understanding of human frailties, and the author is self deprecating about his own achievements.

There are enough rich characterisations and amusing incidents to make a television series. It's a shame that Richard Harris got in first with Outside Edge!

Dick Redbourn has written a book that gets to the very heart and soul of the game at amateur level. It will evoke many memories amongst other cricketers of similar times.

Above all it is a book written, not only with beautiful touches of humour but also in places with great understanding of the aspirations of club cricketer, who occasionally have their moments in the sun, when they make a catch to win the game or strike the winning hit.

Glowing throughout the book is a deep affection for a great game. Dick should be very proud.

February 1996

———◇◇◇◇———

Michael Jayston is a true cricket lover, playing regularly at local level for Rottingdean, and is now the Club's President.

Professionally, a highly experienced and versatile actor, he has appeared in many films and plays over the years, and his best known television roles include: 'The Power game', 'Tinker, Tailor, Soldier, Spy', and 'A bit of a do'. Most appropriately however, he has recently played 'Bob Willis', in the hugely successful TV comedy drama series, 'Outside Edge'.

CHAPTER I

STARDOM?

Having been appointed Archivist and Historian of St. James's C.C. in 1968, I don't think anyone ever mentioned the subject thereafter. Until twenty years later that is, when an enthusiastic Vice-President asked me to produce a full length book on the Club's history for the Centenary in 1998.

Of course the idea was a non-starter; there wasn't sufficient material to write a serious factual tome, unless I copied out every available scorebook, and that would hardly make riveting reading, even for the most dedicated Club follower.

But having hung up my boots, I needed something to keep me in touch with my old pals, so I could natter on, interminably, about the good old days. After months of pondering I dreamt up an audacious idea, the arrogance of which set me chuckling to myself; as a second rate club player and amateur scribbler, why not pen my cricketing autobiography?

All this fevered thought took place around my fiftieth birthday in 1990, when I looked back with great nostalgia to my previous forty summers, almost every weekend of which was dominated by my involvement with the game. It would after all, be an inexpensive and harmless hobby, and fascinating challenge for my middle age, to try and fashion a book from my reminiscences of the cricket I've played in Brighton Parks and Club grounds throughout Sussex.

Apart from my self-indulgence however, there had to be reasons why the outside world might be interested in such a book. Not a natural salesman but dare I suggest, the great library of the game is hardly stacked with biographies of club cricketers, with its chance to share the sheer fun and cameraderie we've enjoyed in our playing days. And this a real flight of fantasy; it might be of interest to a future historian to build a picture of how the club game was really played, during the height of the post war boom, or second golden age.

As a writer, my qualifications for this task can readily be summarised as next to nil. As a club cricketer I've a little more going for me, in that I've played at least a thousand matches at various levels from rock bottom upwards. And, as my occupation of the crease was usually brief, I reckon I've spent at least ninety-five percent of my playing time, literally, observing the game at grassroots level.

Without concern for literary merit, I shall try to set down my fond memories of the characters, anecdotes and humour of the game, which gave me so much pleasure in my playing days. By concentrating on the humour, I hope this book will be enjoyed by a wider audience than my few remaining pals, whose ears I've bashed so relentlessly over the years.

In order to set the scene for later chapters, it's necessary to skip briefly through the 'highlights' of my schooldays and subsequent club cricket career, and sketch the main grounds where much of the action took place.

As a child of the last pre-television generation, I played at cricket and football in the streets and local park for hours every day from an early age. There was nothing much else to do. All this activity taught me something about the game, if only the basic idea of ball control, essential to avoid breaking windows.

I believe my first visit to a big match as a ten year old, was to the County Ground Hove, when Sussex entertained the mighty 1950 West Indians. Then a major event in the local calendar, I was taken there by my Dad, a keen cricket supporter, and we arrived well before the start.

The Ground was already packed, all seats taken, long before we got there. We stood near the nets and people were perched on back garden walls or anywhere they could find. I saw next to nothing of the play; I was too short to see over the spectators and too heavy to sit, for more than a few seconds, on my Dad's shoulders.

The Windies batted first and, I gathered, rapidly took control of events. Before the days of a public address system, rumours about what was going to happen swept round the Ground by hoarse whisper, at great speed. One I particularly remember, as the scoring rate was climbing rapidly, was the forlorn; 'They're going to try James Langridge'.

Incidents from similar occasions remain hazily in mind. Of when Sussex played the '53 Australians, and I managed to jam my head between the hips of two spectators in the front row, having seen little all day. Goggle eyed, I watched in the tense silence as Lindwall bowled the first over of the Sussex innings, to John Langridge.

Even at that tender age, I was totally impressed by his smooth, effortless action, and remember the crisp thwack as each ball hit Langley's gloves. John had a habit of sliding his bat towards the crease as the bowler ran in, before starting his backlift. He did just that to all six balls but, intentionally or otherwise, got no further.

Then I was in a packed throng for the Bank holiday match against Middlesex. The excitement was tangible as Compton went in, and I stretched and craned to catch a glimpse of the action to little avail. As he dashed off a quick 80, frustratingly, I only recall the frequent 'oos' and 'ahs' of the crowd, as they expressed their appreciation of his artistry.

These fleeting experiences of the big time played a vital part in my conversion to cricket addiction. I took away the clear sensations of excitement and tension, plus the vague realisation that the game was a highly technical and complicated affair.

In my last year at Primary School a traumatic event occurred in my sporting development, which shaped my fate as a cricketer. The teacher decided to hold a debate, and called for proposers and opposers for the motion; 'Football is a better game than Cricket'.

There was a hatful of potential proposers, but no-one was interested in the opposition role so, inexplicably, I put my hand up to be immediately appointed the official opposer.

I rushed home to my Dad, firstly to find out what a debate was, then to get his help in preparing my speech. Spotting his chance to do the parental thing, he got carried away, scribbling pages of draft text. As he made no attempt to explain what he was doing, I just left him to get on with it. He then made me read the final text, and taught me some of the basic skills of public speaking; raising the voice, waiting for applause, emphasising points and so on.

On the great day I was very nervous, but when my turn came I launched into my speech with gusto, reading carefully from the prepared text. Unforgettably, this included the sentence:

'Cricket enables the individual to develop, express and fulfil his character, within the context of a team game'.

As I finished that I peered over my paper, to see the whole class including the teacher, staring at me in open mouthed amazement.

The motion was carried almost unanimously, and from that point not only did I become a cricketer, but was also classified as an egg-head, unable to converse in everyday language. Pigeon-holed in this way, I was automatically selected to open the batting when the School played matches, so, like it or not, I'd become a cricketer and batsman.

When I arrived at Varndean Grammar School, I was equipped to launch my cricket career at this level by reputation only. Varndean had a strong sporting tradition, with soccer and cricket teams at every year up to sixteen, plus School First and Second XI's. Almost everyone played sport of some kind, and anyone who didn't, was regarded as 'a bit queer' in the old-fashioned sense of the word.

Having said that, there wasn't much competition for places in the cricket teams, so I played in one side or another each year, reaching the School First XI by the sixth form.

I'd hoped to receive proper coaching from someone suitably qualified, but it turned out that the most knowledgeable cricketers on the staff, were the Sportsmaster Noel Jones, and his colleague Jimmy Foster. Though top class club players, both were off-spin bowlers and tail-end batsmen, so what batting coaching I received, 'left something to be desired'.

An example of this was Noel's oft repeated instruction to, 'get right forward'. Apparently his only notion of defensive play, it led me to thrust my left leg too far down the pitch, off balance. In club cricket later, this basic fault meant I was bowled through the gate dozens of times, before someone pointed out the error of my ways.

Playing top class club cricket, Noel's enthusiasm for the game, and his own performance, were usefully bolstered by his role as Sportsmaster and coach. His Physical Education periods, normally expected to involve some strenuous exercise, were used as another opportunity to hone his spin bowling.

He would whirl away unchanged throughout the period, with a tennis ball, to a batsman wielding a shaven down bat, surrounded by thirty eager close fielders. Survival was limited to a few deliveries; the best technique was to drive hard over the ball, making contact on the downswing. But the combination of spin, bounce and half-bat, ensured Noel would run through the whole class in the forty minute period – well at least everyone got a bat!

In eight years cricket at Varndean, I can only recall one minor incident when I was about sixteen. The coaching sessions for several weeks had concentrated on holding a bat, with leading left hand only, then swinging it up vertical, and down straight through the line of the ball. As someone who's always used too much right hand, it was a timely and useful exercise.

In the next School match, on a soft, wet pitch and with this coaching much in mind, I faced a ball which was short but on off stump. I picked the bat right up, then suddenly realised the ball was skidding through faster and lower than I expected. With prospect of being castled ingloriously with bat aloft, I managed to hurry the blade down straight and make contact.

I middled what I thought was an adequate backward defensive, till I saw the non-striker a few yards away, screaming at me to run. Startled, I looked up just in time to see the ball race over the boundary between cover and extra, before I could leave the crease.

After careful consideration through the many years since, and without undue self-effacement, I'm convinced that that shot was the only time I've ever timed a stroke perfectly!

I shall always be grateful to Noel Jones, part of whose consuming passion for the game communicated itself to me. And with hindsight, he could spin a ball faster than anyone I've ever played with since; I still remember a newish ball fizzing through the air when facing him in a School match.

Though technically ill-equipped, by the end of my schooldays I was still raring to get out into the big, wide world of club cricket, optimistically believing there were thousands of runs to be plundered.

In my last School year I took my first step in that direction, when Noel Jones asked me to turn out for Brighton and Hove, to make up the numbers. The Club was, and remains, one of the strongest in Sussex, and I played mostly mid-week, against tough opposition scattered around the County and beyond.

Cricket-wise I'd been thrown in at the deep end. My memory now was of a long, hot summer, with a lot of hard chasing, and occasionally doing deep square at both ends. Put in at number nine on merit, only five or six batsmen were usually needed, so I didn't get much practice at the crease.

It was an instructive and tough introduction to competitive club cricket but, though everyone was very friendly, I didn't overly enjoy the experience. On the plus side, I was introduced to club cricket humour, and picked up one of my favourite phrases, much used since. We'd all crowded round the Team Secretary at the end of a game, to get details of the next match. At a time when I didn't even own a push-bike, his instructions were short and sharp:

'The game is at Ashford, two fifteen start, make your own way there!'

It's a lovely all-purpose throw-away line for anyone who doesn't know, or can't be bothered to sort out, the travelling arrangements.

I went up to Durham University in '59, and in the summer term was uncertain whether to play cricket or not. To help make up my mind, I went to watch the First XI in action at the Racecourse Ground. Having seen a few overs, I enquired about the Second and Third XI's, but there weren't any. That removed any thoughts of University cricket.

During the holidays my father, then Secretary of St. James's, passed word I was keen to play the odd game if they were short, on the strict understanding I wasn't good enough to play at that level. Though correct, it hardly bolstered morale, and I almost dreaded the call to turn out.

When it came I was extremely self-conscious, well aware that I was mixing with much more experienced and skilful cricketers. But I was drawn to the Club by the warmth of the welcome and the pervading sense of fun. Skipper David Benjamin especially, tried hard to keep me in the game, praised any good play, and did his best to build my confidence.

It was also my initiation into the art of beer drinking, and recall being staggered at the rate pints were downed after a match. Until then, I'd had no reason to drink more than the odd half, and found the speed at which fresh pints were plonked in front of me quite daunting.

As a student I wasn't expected to buy a round, and had no problem in convincing myself it was bad manners to reject the generosity of others. However, it still took me several years of hard practice, before I raised my consumption rate to that acceptable for a proper club cricketer.

In the '62 season I was unable to return to Durham because of a winter illness, so I looked for any games of cricket I could find. Through friends on the staff of Brighton Corporation, I turned out as a guest for the Brighton Council XI, then captained and dominated by one Alderman Percy Friend-James. Those matches remain the most hilarious and farcical I've ever seen, and I've tried to chronicle events as faithfully as possible in a later chapter.

When I finished at Durham, I resumed living in Brighton while commuting to London for my first job. For cricket, I played for the Old Varndeanians on Saturdays and NALGO on Sundays, both teams being based in Preston Park. Built at the turn of the century, the Park became the centre of club cricket in Brighton between the Wars, and representative matches were arranged against the Hove equivalent, the County Ground.

The Park is a flat, circular area about 200 yards in diameter, surrounded by a cycle track with terraces, paths, a brick pavilion and a wooden stand. At that time, demand for pitches was near the peak of the post-war boom, so the playing area was divided up to allow four matches to take place at once. I will attempt to explain how the boundaries for each match were drawn, though this may well be beyond my powers of description and geometry.

The circle was split into north and south semi-circles, and a wide cricket table was developed near the centre of each half. Then two parallel pitches were cut on each table, separated by as wide a margin as possible.

The boundary for a particular match would then be: the adjacent quarter circumference of the cycle track, an imaginary line drawn through the middle stumps of the parallel pitch, and an infinitely extended bowling crease through the nearer wickets of each pitch in the other semi-circle. This arrangement produced a reasonable playing area for each match, but could pose frightful problems for outfielders, as I describe later.

The pavilion was inadequate for eighty-eight players, so half were banished to a basement changing room under the wooden stand, not providing much of a view of the action. Inside the pavilion there were locker benches all round with about thirty clothes pegs, and a small tea-room at one end. There were also two small washbasins, but as they were used as a shelf for the practice nets, there was no running water within the changing area.

In fact, anyone in need of a wash or toilet, had to walk across to the public conveniences nearby, with coin in hand. It was also noticeable that, in an age before male deodorants, anyone making a big score would leave the ground on a high, in more senses than one.

Another irritating feature of the pavilion was its frosted glass windows. With fixed bottom sashes, it meant no-one could watch the games from inside, without climbing onto a sill to poke head out the top. Most players therefore, sat on a bench on the cycle track or edge of the playing area.

In spite of these minor drawbacks, great enthusiasm for the game was generated in a buzz of activity on a Saturday afternoon. One of the golden rules was to arrive early enough to commandeer a peg, otherwise, double pegged there was real risk of losing one's trousers. Also, one had to bear in mind that the tea intervals were staggered, to ease the pressure on the over-worked tea ladies. If your match was last, it was essential to be first in the queue or there'd be nothing left.

When the action started, there'd be a sprawling scrum around the pavilion of fielders, batsmen, officials and spectators, from all four matches. As most of the teams knew each other they made an informal Preston Park cricket society, and match details were passed around, everyone keeping their eyes on the most exciting game.

I enjoyed fielding in the Park because if my own match was boring, there'd be three others to watch, equivalent to zapping in the TV era. Yet years on, nightmarish memories still linger of the technique necessary for survival in certain fielding positions.

The fun started if you were posted to deep square leg between parallel pitches, which meant you stood only yards from the wicket of the adjacent match. Experienced players would cope with this by watching both games and, as bowlers rarely delivered the ball at the

Preston Park, with multi-match cricket in progress

same instant, could quickly switch their gaze from match to match. But on average every twenty minutes or so, the hair raising scenario occurred when both bowlers reached their wickets in unison.

The technique I developed was to squat low on my haunches, hands clamped behind head, which would be pulled hard down between my knees. As compact as possible, this would just allow me to peer out under my eyebrows to watch my match. I remember feeling the heat of fright and tension rising up through my head, as the bowlers reached the stumps.

By presenting only my heels, backside and lower back to the batsman behind me, I reckoned any injury received would be painful rather than fatal. Generally this worked but, if the dangers of this weren't enough, one could also get paranoid about being struck by a lofted drive, from the other semi-circle of the Park. Even at a fairly tender age, I adopted a fatalistic view on that one.

Things could also be quite lively for spectators or others. For example, a ball struck for six south of the Pavilion would sail over a tall hedge before descending onto tennis courts at a lower level. As the players couldn't see the ball coming till the last moment, it was like playing in an air raid, yet they kept going fearlessly.

Likewise, sixes to the north end could clear the low perimeter wall and rain down on traffic in the busy Preston Drove. When this happened, everyone would hold their breath and listen carefully for the impact. A thud onto tarmac brought a sigh of relief, but a metallic clunk caused the public spirited to rush to assist, and the squeamish to slink away.

Talking of sixes in Preston Park, there's a lovely anecdote about a game played there towards the end of the War, when a local side entertained a visiting Royal Australian Air Force XI. Prominent in the home XI was Keith Wilson, brother of the founder of St. James's C.C., and probably the finest Sussex club cricketer of his generation. With the local side fielding, Keith was tossing up his flighty leg-breaks when a certain Keith Ross Miller came out to bat. Bored after a few overs of knocking the bowling around, he said to the wicketkeeper:

'I'm going to try something next ball; keep your head down.'

As the ball was in the air, Miller walked down the off side to where it would pitch, raising his bat as he did so. Then he spun round behind the ball and straight drove it, back over the 'keeper's head and sightscreen for six.

I don't know if the 'keeper had a heart attack on the spot, or later, when he'd had time to think about it.

After several seasons playing home matches in Preston Park, usually opening the batting, I became almost a 'star' performer at this level of the game – the term 'star' has special significance which I clarify later. I played around 50 matches a season, every Saturday and Sunday, plus any available mid-week, evening, or Bank holidays fixtures.

In true club cricket tradition, I never kept a proper tally of the runs I scored, but got quite excited one season when I reckoned I'd got about 1100. I was quite chuffed about this, casually mentioning it to my mates at every opportunity. But when I checked the scorebooks again, and found I'd played no less than 52 innings, I decided to drop the subject.

The evening games I played, mostly in East Brighton Park on a Wednesday, were a prime example of the tremendous enthusiasm for cricket at that time. Teams would rush to the ground after work, to try and get the game started as soon after six o'clock as possible. Matches were 20 overs a side and, later in the season, if the game started too late, it could be almost dark by the last few overs.

Though it may have looked like a knockabout, there were some good club players involved and with overs per bowler unlimited, it was often a hard fought, well balanced contest. I remember one such game when the first side scored 192 for 5, and the opposition got them with an over to spare.

A lasting impression of these games was that of the failing light at the end. One incident I recall clearly was when ten runs were wanted from the last over in, essentially, semi-darkness.

A ball was thrashed high to long-off where the fielder, apparently watching it carefully, moved a few yards across into the line of flight. Then without moving his arms, or attempting the catch, the ball flew over his shoulder a few inches from his face, for six. He stood there, ashen faced and speechless, as it dawned on him how close he'd come to a nasty injury.

There was a dead keen chap called Sam, I remember, who filled in for my team from week to week, and was desperately keen to become a cricketer. Unfortunately he was almost entirely lacking in talent, basic skills, and any hint of athleticism. Intentionally or otherwise, he looked like an unfit 'WG', with full blown figure, thick black beard, small cap, and ancient buckskin boots.

It was always a problem where to put him in the field as he couldn't run at much more than walking pace. In this all-action cricket, he couldn't race about the outfield, he couldn't catch the ball either, so slips or close field were out, leaving only mid-on or mid-off. Sam would stand there with heels of boots together and feet at right angles; if the batsman drove into the vee, great, otherwise it would pass by unhindered.

Sam was an equal embarrassment when we were batting, incapable of making contact with the ball, and as a non-runner unable to take any quick singles. But the skipper had to get him in the game somehow, so would initially put him at seven or eight. Invariably, if a close finish looked like developing and Sam was next in, the skipper would shuffle the order, to put a better player in before him.

After demotion like this for several weeks, Sam would get uptight about the situation, and threaten to make himself unavailable unless given a proper chance. After this 'discussion' had taken place one day, Sam was put at five with a firm promise from the skipper he'd stay there come what may.

We started the game batting well enough, and after ten overs had lost two wickets with Sam due in next. Sitting in the pavilion, padded up, gloves on, he couldn't believe his luck when there was a clap of thunder and a curtain of heavy rain swept across the ground. In abject misery he remained there motionless, as the rest of us got changed to go down the pub.

By the mid '60's, I found myself increasingly drawn towards St. James's, with more opportunities to play as they extended their Sunday fixture list. With an attractive home ground at Stanmer Park, it seemed to be a Club with a longer history, better social life, and higher standard of cricket. However small my contribution, I immensely enjoyed playing with Peter Beecheno, Derek Pickering, John Moore, David Atkins and others, all top class club cricketers - at their best not far below county level.

My team mates in St. James's introduced me to 'Ossie' Osborne, and enabled me to get some mid-week games with Brighton Brunswick, one of the most prestigious Clubs in the County. Though out of my depth at that level, it was an eye-opener in several ways, and I've described some of my experiences with the Brunswick in a later chapter.

With all home matches for St. James's and Brighton Council XI played in Stanmer Park, this then became the focus of my cricketing activities. Stanmer was undoubtedly the most attractive of the Corporation grounds, and I've often seen artists making paintings, or sketches, of the scene at its best.

The approach road off the Lewes Road winds up, for half a mile, through scattered clumps of trees, before sweeping left of the playing area, to pass in front of the House. It then circles round the church and pond, forming the boundary opposite the House, before rejoining the main drive.

Stanmer House is an 18th century stone building used, when I played, by a department of Sussex University. With the House on the south side, Stanmer church is to the west, with a pond and overhanging elm tree in a north-west position. (Unfortunately the elm tree had to be cut down during the '80's, which much diminishes the scene.)

Opposite the House on the north side, is a meadow used for grazing, on a slope with knots of trees. More trees each side of the approach road on the eastern side, completed the scene which, given appropriate weather, could produce a superb setting for a cricket match.

From the playing angle, the main, and fairly fundamental drawback to this scenic splendour, was the absence of a pavilion. Players were obliged to walk up a path through trees to change in an old stable block to the side of the House, also doubling as the groundsman's store.

Clambering up an outside iron staircase, there were three small, wooden rooms, each with splintered, bare floors, and equipped with half a dozen pegs and three benches. When I first played, there were two basins with cold water only, and the toilet was an outside urinal, screened by a woven wood fence.

The small playing area, originally the lawn in front of the House, has the table level roughly the same as the pond. With the absence of heavy rolling, or perhaps any rolling, a typical Stanmer pitch was slow and over-grassed, with the ball tending to stop and lift. Only after a long dry spell would it come through at a pace where it could be safely driven on the front foot.

By the '66 season I was firmly established as a St. James's player, occasionally putting together a few runs in the middle order, and this period marked the peak of my enthusiasm for playing the game.

It seems ridiculous now, but we even went through with our scheduled fixture against Old Grammarians at Stanmer, on the day of the World Cup Final. Someone rigged up a 12 inch black and white portable television, operated from a car battery, in one of the changing rooms, giving a flickering, grainy picture.

Both sides were anxious, praying even, to win the toss and bat first, but we lost and I missed seeing most of normal time. With tension becoming unbearable in extra time, cricket was suspended by mutual agreement, and everyone packed into the changing room to watch the drama.

The other unforgettable affair from that year, was the wonderful episode of the quest for Salisbury's 1000 runs.

Tony Salisbury was one of the great characters of local cricket, a stalwart of Rottingdean C.C., who'd played for the Brunswick and many other top sides in his day. A tall, slim 'chap', he was the most generous purveyor of beer I've ever had the good fortune to meet. He'd go down to the Plough after a game, still wearing white flannels and sweater, fill up a jug, and then circulate ceaselessly, topping up everyone's glass as soon as there was a 'hole in it'.

The episode started when we were getting changed for our last match of the season, Sunday 2nd October at Rottingdean. Salisbury made it clear from the outset, he was enjoying his most successful year with the bat, and needed only 73 to complete a thousand runs for the Club for the first time. In the match, his semi-serious requests for a few 'friendly ones' to help him on his way, were laughed off, but he did score 32 before holing out.

In the Plough later for the end of season celebration, it became clear that Salisbury was genuinely disappointed about his failure to reach his thousand. In an inspired move, Peter Beecheno strode to the door, glanced up at the nearly dark sky, and declared authoritively that the weather would be fine the next weekend, so we could arrange another match. With instant mutual agreement, teams were selected on the spot, and Beecheno's XI versus Rottingdean was fixed for Sunday October 9th, one thirty start.

It was in fact a cold bright day, and with well matched sides a hard fought game was contested but, disaster of disasters, when Salisbury got to the wicket he lunged forward and was caught behind first ball. Again in the Plough afterwards, Beecheno predicted with absolute certainty fine weather for the following Sunday the 16th, so much the same sides were selected, with a one o'clock start.

Remarkably, it was indeed another fine day, but with much evidence of dew and five degrees colder. This time Salisbury, visibly shaking with nerves, batted with real application to score 23, leaving him just 18 short of his target. In the Plough afterwards, no spurious weather forecasting was necessary, and arrangements were put in hand for the third game on the 23rd. Some far-sighted soul pointed out that the clocks went back on the 30th so, because of the light, the 23rd would be Salisbury's last chance.

Mike Bowring of Cuckfield, organised the visiting team and, with many regulars involved in winter sport, new faces had to be recruited, a development which nearly undid the whole exercise.

The 23rd was a cold bright day, and with a hard frost the pitch turned out as fast as any we'd played on all season. Starting at twelve thirty, Bowring's XI batted first and scored 95, leaving Rottingdean a comfortable two hours to get the runs. Selecting his order with care, Salisbury thought it safe enough to put himself at three for the Rottingdean innings.

The first sign of trouble was when the openers raced away, and put on over fifty for the first wicket. Then, when Salisbury finally got to the crease, he was ridiculously nervous, prodding and missing at most deliveries, making every bowler look unplayable. It should be added, his performance had not been improved by a hard lunchtime session in the Plough.

We tried hard to feed him every possible rubbishy delivery, and he painfully scraped together a few edgy singles to move into double figures. By this time Rottingdean only needed a dozen to win, so the most complex situation had developed. The bowling side were trying to avoid getting Salisbury out and give him runs, while the other batsman was trying to feed him the bowling, without scoring himself. When still six short, the most hilarious incident took place. One of the new players was a keen chap in his early twenties, something of a 'star' performer with all the kit. Not knowing the background he thought this was a serious match, and as one of nature's competitors, believed in putting one hundred per cent effort into everything.

Salisbury at last plucked up courage to lash out at a ball, but only succeeded in getting a top edge, sending a catch steepling towards the covers, where our young 'star' was patrolling. He quickly got under the ball and started to shuffle about, as it swung around in the air.

Every fielder shouted at him, with varying degrees of hysteria, to 'drop it'. Unable to believe what he was hearing, he kept glancing down from watching the ball, his face contorted with conflicting expressions, as he tried to fathom out if we were serious.

In the end he went flat out to hold the catch, but just failed to do so, finishing by rolling on the ground with the ball a few feet away. Thus reprieved, Salisbury rode his luck to reach his goal to tumultuous applause and audible relief all round.

The match had finished just before the scheduled five-thirty, which meant there was an hour and a half to kill before opening time. More in hope than expectation, a dozen players went down to the Plough, waking the Landlord from his afternoon nap, with a stone to the upstairs window. He quickly made his feelings known but Salisbury, with his in-depth knowledge of medieval licensing law, had his measure.

Pointing out that the Plough was an Inn, he demanded his right to shelter and sustenance as a needy traveller, a suggestion which generated hearty laughter from the landlord. But Salisbury insisted he was deadly serious, demanding a room for the night, and furthermore, wished to book in twelve guests who happened to be standing alongside.

After a bit more argy-bargy, the landlord admitted defeat and reluctantly opened up, to allow us to start the most uninhibited booze up I can remember after a cricket match. I know for a fact we got through nine jugs, about seventy pints, and that was before the normal opening time!

A true sense of euphoria was induced that final evening, as, closetted in the small bar, I reflected we'd defied the weather and shortened the winter, as well as fashioning three extra superb games of cricket. And of course Salisbury, in white flannels and blazer as always, was an extremely happy man.

This episode marked the end of the carefree days, when I simply looked around for any game I could get, and was oblivious to the problems and responsibilities of running a cricket club. It was also around the time I accepted reluctantly I was never likely to progress to a higher level of the game. My ambitions to become a 'star' having run their course, I would steadily become a player who, perhaps subconsciously, put team and club first; someone we later defined as a 'domestic' cricketer.

DOMESTICITY

By my mid twenties, I was becoming more closely involved with St. James's C.C., attracted by the personalities of the leading players, and the off the field activities. This fascination was fuelled by their superior cricketing skills, and I thought somehow, I might pick up tips to improve my own game. In practice, it meant I spent most of my time in the field, or waiting to bat.

I was once given a chance up the order at four, and ended up on three consecutive Saturdays, sitting padded up throughout our innings. But with dog like devotion, I was there every week, just delighted to be part of the scene. I realise now, at a time when St. James's only ran one team, I was a second XI player without a second XI to play for.

The second phase of my career began in '68, when I took on the job of Team Secretary and, a year later, that of Fixture Secretary. At a time when several leading players had just left, the first job was very tough going, and it's safe to say I might have been less keen on the second, had I known I was to hold office for 19 years.

For all that dedicated service, I've never been allowed to forget that in the first flush of enthusiasm, I arranged an emergency fill-in fixture with the Keymer Brick and Tile Company at their ground. None of us had played there before, we had no idea of their strength, so we turned up ready for anything.

We were asked to change in the half-derelict conservatory, at the back of a large country house, and I remember being suspicious because there was no evidence of previous cricket activity. We trooped out to the ground, some fifty yards from the back of the house, which was a fair sized playing area, fully surrounded by tall trees like a forest clearing. Again, there was no sign of cricket having been played; a few benches, a table and a small scoreboard were taken out and were the only equipment on the ground.

If there was a square, its perimeter was not discernible, but a strip had been cut and the surface looked playable. Nonetheless, some of our players thought the whole set-up looked distinctly dodgy, so when the batting order was sorted out, I was instructed to open and face the first ball.

Trying hard to look nonchalant, when the moment came, I pushed forward gingerly to a good length delivery from a slow-medium bowler. The ball stood up and scraped across the top of my head, as I remained frozen in my forward push. Shaken and scared, I faced up to the second ball, which was very short and as I went onto the back foot, shot along the ground to hit me on the instep. Thankfully given out LBW, I retired with haste and relief to the boundary.

In the light of this and similar experiences, we concluded the pitch surface was like a roller-coaster, the bounce depending on whether it hit a down or up slope. A conference was called, and the technique agreed was to get well outside the line of the ball and play everything with a cross bat. This tactic, allied to our greater skill at rounders, enabled us to win in the end.

The '69 season marked a distinct trough in the affairs of the Club, two stalwarts having left the area, we were left with only six players who'd turn out for both weekend games, plus eight who'd do one game only.

Naively, having taken the job of Team Secretary, I was faced with the daunting task of finding eleven for each match on a fixture list, recently expanded to include most Sundays. It was my toughest time in club cricket, as I made dozens of calls every week imploring Vice-Presidents, retired players and acquaintances in other clubs, to turn out. By the end of the season I was mentally exhausted, and thankful to duck out of the task the following year.

So far in this tale, I've been appropriately self-effacing about my batting performances but, given favourable conditions and weak opposition, I could plunder a few runs as well as the next man. In all the gloom of the '69 season, the one high point for me was when I scored my first century. In theory every shot should be indelibly etched on my mind, but in fact I can only recall the amusing moments.

The match was at the Rotary Ground Worthing and the opposition, Worthing Chippingdale, were weak on the day. It was a bright dry September afternoon and, with little rain in the previous week, both wicket and close cut outfield were hard and fast.

Puttie, my favourite character and subject of a later chapter, was skipper for the day, and when he won the toss and batted, opened with John Moore and Ian Boyd-Pain, with me at three. First luck came as we got ready; B-P had launched into one of his long-winded shaggy dog stories, and was still padding up when the openers were due to go out. Puttie gave me the nod and I nipped in to open with John Moore.

From the first over the bowling looked friendly, and we were soon scoring more or less as we liked. It appeared that Chippingdale had only two regular bowlers, both slow-medium, and the supporting fielding was hardly dynamic. In their opening spells they bowled tidily enough, but as the after-noon wore on and they tired, they became little more than cannon fodder.

I reached my fifty with a square cut four when, with the whole off-side field round the boundary except cover, one of them contrived to let the ball through his legs, when it had almost stopped.

To the next delivery, adrenalin flowing, confidence sky high, I lashed out head in the air, trying to knock the cover off the ball. It was a dreadful front foot ya-hoo, which connected high on the outside edge, sending the ball in a gentle arc, no more than twenty feet high, straight towards the solitary cover fielder. He could have caught it by closing his eyes and putting his hands together, but instead turned the task into a display of acrobatics.

He'd lost concentration – not surprising as most of the off-side shots had been struck violently past him – when he'd suddenly woken up to the fact an easy catch was coming his way. Reacting instinctively by sprinting a couple of paces to his left, he then picked up the flight and jack-knifed back, diving horizontally through his starting point.

Sailing through the air like a goalkeeper at full stretch, he clutched the ball to his stomach with both hands, before landing on the point of his right elbow. Spilling the ball as he did so, he then rolled about in genuine agony, while onlookers were unsure whether to laugh or cry. It was one of the most spectacular dropped catches I've seen, and allowed me to calm down, while the poor fellow was helped off the field.

I then advanced haphazardly to my century, surviving another dropped chance, and assisted by being fed the bowling. The last twenty came quickly, arguably, 'in a blaze of strokeplay'. This period contained an incident which I would tentatively suggest was unique, and my only claim to wider cricketing fame.

Puttie, through lack of a volunteer, was forced to do the scoring and, hard pressed to keep up with the torrent of runs, blew a red-hot cinder from his pipe onto the scorebook. I suggest therefore, I'm the only batsman in the history of the game, to both literally and metaphorically, 'have set the scorebook alight'.

In '70, for a variety of reasons, we moved from Brighton to Crowborough. Logically I should have joined the local Club, but being so involved with St. James's, I decided to continue playing for them. In practical terms it meant travelling the 25 miles or so to the Brighton area, with no home matches. Also, like most club cricketers I'm a sentimentalist, and was reluctant to leave 'my own' Club and pals.

In that first year away from my home patch, I suffered the one nasty injury I've received playing cricket, though nothing to get too excited about. Playing against Bexhill at the Polegrove one Sunday, I went in at number five when we were in urgent need of quick runs. Tony Pooley, a bowler who knew all about line and length, had tied up one end for some time, and I had the task of sorting him out.

After several maidens had slipped by, I became desperate to score runs, but simply didn't have the talent and technique to score against someone of his accuracy. Eventually in sheer frustration, I tried to hook a ball I judged to be short, but in fact was not much different to the previous deliveries.

The shot was hopelessly late, the ball hitting my mouth on the lower jaw, pushing four front teeth back to the horizontal. There was no blood, it didn't hurt much, and I left the field in a reasonably dignified way.

Someone found a dentist, and I was supposed to be pleased when he announced the teeth had broken cleanly within the gums. But being England on a Sunday, nothing could be done till the next day. Memorably, I drove home feeling sorry for myself, but at least certain of tea and sympathy from my wife Carol. Her exact words of greeting as I stepped in the door were, 'Good God; what's happened to you? You look like Dracula!'

The early '70's marked a period of fascination with what might loosely be called the intellectual side of the game. No longer too concerned about my own performances, I started to pay more attention to the idiosyncrasies of my colleagues. With no shortage of like-minded people in the Club, we developed an intense interest in the humorous aspects of the game at our level.

Initial material was provided by the division between the public schoolboys, called the 'chaps', and the state schoolboys, known as 'yobs'. With the Club membership split fairly evenly, there was a feast of opportunities for sarcastic humour. Virtually any misdemeanour, however minor, was pounced on and the offender chided with, 'typical of a chaps behaviour' or, 'entirely what one would expect from a yob'. This provided staple fare for several seasons, and we even advanced into the abstruse area of the 'chob'; someone who had attended both public and state schools.

We also came to the conclusion that, the regular players in most club cricket teams can be broadly divided into two groups, leaving aside non-cricketers. The concept of a 'star' performer was already well established, and could broadly be defined as someone who had often played, and could be expected to play, a significant role in a match.

But in club cricket there are, in practice, only limited opportunities for stardom. The batting time per side is around two and a half hours, and at best only three batsmen have time to build a proper innings, the late order left to have a quick swing before tea. Likewise, two good opening bowlers can easily reel off over half the total overs bowled, before the first change is made.

It follows therefore, as well as the 'stars' there has to be another category of club cricketer, which we named the 'domestics'. They would not expect to play a significant role in a match, but be content with an unselfish, supporting role, yet still enjoy playing the game. Over the months we learned to recognise both types, and analysed the characteristics in minute detail, providing much fun for all. We reached a level of sophistication whereby we could pigeon hole the entire opposition within minutes of them arriving at the ground, and well before seeing them in action.

Our full definition of a 'star', more recently hyped to 'super-star' and 'mega-star', was someone with self-confidence and talent, strengthened by his track record, which led him to be sure of making runs or taking wickets in most circumstances. He would be modest, rarely discussing his performances, past or present, and would feign disinterest in scores and averages.

Typically, a star would own a full set of kit, including pads, showing signs of wear without being tatty. He would possess more than one sweater and cap, all being contained in a proper cricket bag, preferably initialled. Anyone sporting a cricket 'coffin' would win automatic 'star' status, a spare pair of pads strapped to the outside suggesting 'megastar' classification. Presenting a laid back image, underneath, a 'star' would be concerned about his performance and reputation, and usually make efforts to keep himself and kit in reasonable shape.

The other category of club cricketer, we felt, had been undervalued and unidentified, yet was an essential member of the team. Tony DaVall suggested that non-'star' players should be named after the French term 'domestiques', which applied to the journeyman members of cycle racing teams. 'Domestiques' would set the pace, shield the 'star' rider and obstruct the opposition, doing everything in their power to set up a victory for their top man, while foregoing all chance of glory themselves.

'Domesticity' creeps up on a player, when the state of mind develops that he no longer expects to play a major role in a match. With reduced ambitions, apathy sets in, and he accepts his place as an essential, but unglamorous, part of the team. A 'domestic' batsman expects the 'stars' to perform, knowing he is most likely to be called into serious action, only if the opposition bowlers, or the pitch, are unplayable. Similarly, the 'domestic' bowler will only be brought on if, the 'stars' get too tired, have been knocked about, or the score is 190 for one twenty minutes before tea.

A 'domestic's' kit will usually be in a state of decay, with studless uncleaned boots, ancient pimpled rubber gloves, ill-fitting sweaters either shrunk to the waist or stretched to knee level, smelly mis-matched socks and unhygienic jock-strap. All this would be thrown into at best, a battered old-fashioned cricket bag, at worst, a small dog-eared holdall.

We identified numerous clues when classifying players, self-confidence being a vital sign. For example, a modern fad for in-going batsmen is to whirl the bat around to loosen up, a give away when sorting out 'stars' and 'domestics'. A 'star' would carry out the exercise with authority, warning the fielding side of troubles ahead. Conversely, the 'domestic' would either, lack the nerve to do it, or look self conscious and unconvincing if he did.

With chaps, yobs, stars and domestics, the repartee in the pavilion reached a level of sophistication I've never experienced before or since. It was a stimulating and immensely enjoyable phase in my cricketing life, created by the inventiveness of those involved. With phrases like 'star chap opener', 'middle-aged domestic trundler', 'has-been chap super-star', being bandied around, an outsider over-hearing would have little idea what we were talking about.

We had in the changing room a superb mix of characters, all trying to upstage each other verbally. To summarise individual styles I would suggest: Derek Pickering, corinthian purist; Peter Withers, erudite literary schoolmaster; Tony DaVall, incisive intellectual; Mark Whitlock, frustrated aspiring star; Peter Gaskell, disorganised talent; Nick Wright, laconic wit; and Ian Boyd-Pain, charismatic bullshit star. Then of course, sucking on his pipe in the background, would be dear old Puttie, the ultimate gentleman domestic. He would come up with what he thought was a sparkling comment from time to time, to be instantly ridiculed by everyone.

This rich vein of humour lasted for several seasons and I decided to test its effect on a wider audience by writing a spoof memorandum about 'stars' and 'domestics' which I sent to Derek Pickering. Containing exaggerated examples of the genre, Derek read the memo to the Club's Stag Dinner in '74. Though dated now, I quote below the main section defining the categories.

STAR STATUS:

Generally a cricketer is a 'star' if he expects to bat and score runs and/or bowl and take wickets. He is therefore in a position to influence the course of a match.

A STAR BATSMAN:

Always expects to bat in the first six.

Draws a line with his boot when taking guard.

Wears a box.

Owns his own bat.

Always gets a dodgy decision if given L.B.W.

Never misses a straight ball, but plays down the wrong line.

Sulks if run out.

Weeps and rages if run out by a domestic batsman.

Never swings or tonks but strokes and pushes the ball about.

May refuse to play on certain dicey tracks.

Calls for a glass of water when he reaches 50.

A STAR BOWLER:

Is always 'there or thereabouts'.

Paces out his run-up.

Has studs in his boots and peels off his sweater.

Has frequent trouble with his foothold.

Always has a red mark on his flannels.

Knows what sawdust is for.

Breaks down if knocked about by a star batsman.

Limps off in agony with a twisted ankle if knocked about by a domestic batsman.

DOMESTIC STATUS:

A domestic cricketer does not expect to influence the course of the game, therefore bats or bowls only when necessary and knows his place.

A DOMESTIC BATSMAN:

Often asks for 'middle from where 'e bowls'.

Always edges the ball.

Gropes forward at least once an over and 'ya-hoos' frequently.

Cannot run more than 2 to any shot.

Falls over when sweeping.

Runs down the middle of the wicket and often collides with the other batsman.

May take a quick 'drag' between overs.

A DOMESTIC BOWLER:

Generally pitches within a radius of 10 yards of the batsman.

Wears a short-sleeved shirt.

Does warming up exercises after bowling a wide.

Appeals ecstatically if the batsman misses a ball.

Expects to be taken off after each over.

Calls a 'donkey drop' his slower ball.

Consequent to the above a domestic spends most of his time in the field and in this department he:

Is not expected to catch the ball.

Proceeds after the ball at a gentle trot.

Lobs the ball back in a graceful arc.

Often gets hit in the 'privates' when backing up.

Collides with a star who was about to make a great catch.

Probably fields at fine leg both ends.

Chats amicably with the square leg umpire.

In addition to the above a domestic cricketer:

Has to be early for a match in order to do the chores.

Never cleans his boots or may wear dirty plimsolls

Only speaks to a star when spoken to.

Always buys drinks for the stars.

Has to take the 'missus' home early.

Thinks a box is a 2 foot cube of cardboard.

Never gets the spare crumpet.

This first reading of the 'Memo' went down extremely well with the eighty-odd diners, who quickly appreciated the concept, and roared with laughter at most of the lines. I was particularly pleased to see those who had not heard the idea before, rapidly cottoning on and appreciating the joke. It strengthened my belief that 'domesticity' might be appreciated by a wider audience.

Having played club cricket for around fifteen years, it also occurred to me that, as friends with lengthy shared experience, we had built up dozens of stories and anecdotes which we re-told time and again. If I could write them up in a readable way, allied to 'domesticity', it could make the basis of a humorous book.

I set out to do just that, in a starry-eyed way, convinced I would achieve over-night fame and, more important, fortune. My major technical problem, apart from having no training or experience as a writer, was to link together all the disparate incidents and people, and form a coherent text, rather than just a list of unconnected items. Undaunted, I produced a first draft in under a year, then played around changing bits for a few months, ending up with 40,000 words of moderately grammatical text.

About this time, I was delighted to read in the Sunday Times, a report of a Warwickshire match by Norman Harris, who contrasted Rohan Kanhai as a 'star', and Neal Abberley as a 'domestique'. I sent him a copy of my 'Memo', effectively saying 'stars' and 'domestics' were a well established concept, and if he wanted a fuller understanding, please read the attached.

He liked the idea and wrote a long article, quoting most of my 'Memo' verbatim, which appeared on the back page on August 29th '76. I was chuffed about this, and irritated that none of my friends saw it. The reason I found out was that I'd been sent a copy by a friend up north, and it only appeared in the first overseas, and north of England editions!

With no idea how to get a book published, I drew up a list of well-known publishers, penned a polite letter and sent off the draft to each in turn. These were always returned with a standard rejection slip, sometimes it appeared, with unseemly haste.

Stumbling on like this for months, I was eventually introduced to Ian Morley-Clarke, who ran a small company, Midas Books, based at Speldhurst near Tunbridge Wells. Ian greatly enjoyed the draft and understood precisely what I was getting at, having played the game at every level from Minor Counties downwards. After taking other opinions he agreed to publish, with the object of having the book available for the start of the '77 season.

When that decision was taken in early November '76, I was delegated the tasks of finding a willing celebrity to write the foreword, produce photographs or illustrations, and dream up an eye-catching front cover.

By luck, just about the biggest celebrity in the land at that time was Tony Greig, captain of Sussex and England, and I could at least claim to have played a club match with him, when he first came over from South Africa. He was hardly a bosom pal, but Derek Pickering and Don Bates agreed to see him on my behalf, to ask if he would write or sanction a foreword.

Unfortunately, by the time they pinned him down, it was the day before he had to leave with the England team for the winter tour of India and Pakistan. Though his thoughts must have been elsewhere, he saw the funny side of the book – or said he did – and readily agreed to the foreword, leaving details to be sorted out with his agent.

I was grateful for Tony Greig's positive response on this matter, trivial to him, important to me. But there was an amusing – or depressing – postscript to his involvement. Ian Morley-Clarke was delighted about the Greig foreword and decided to trumpet the fact on the front cover. Some months later, on the very day the books were available for distribution from the printers, Greig was sacked in shame from the England captaincy, because of the Packer affair.

Next on the agenda was the photographs, and some were available from scrapbooks and Club archives. But we needed some shots specifically relating to 'stars' and 'domestics', so we set up a couple of sessions with an old pal John Hindmarsh, a keen amateur photographer.

To get an exaggerated portrait of Tony DaVall as a 'domestic' we found some dilapidated kit – not too difficult – to add to ill-fitting clothing, and took shots from every angle. For the 'star' portrait we asked Ian Boyd-Pain to put on his usual kit and act naturally. For additional effect we told him to wear a white neckerchief, and within seconds we had the perfect photograph.

For the key front cover photo, I decided the most eye-catching would be a close-up of a 'domestic' groping forward, and getting bowled. A session was arranged in late November at Fulking, the Preston Nomads ground, which turned out to be as amateurish as the subject matter. To start with, only Derek Pickering and Ian Boyd-Pain turned up, so we had three players plus the photographer on the ground.

A bonus was that by then the outfield was like a meadow, and the table, uncut for weeks, enhanced the rural, 'grass roots' image. By skilful use of our resources, we got the secondary shots we wanted before concentrating our efforts on the cover photo.

B-P padded up as 'keeper, and was instructed to wear a cap and keep his head down, so he wouldn't be recognised from the 'star' portrait. A ball was taped to the off stump and I posed in the most exaggerated groping position.

The selected shot conveyed the grope well enough, but it was amazing how many readers thought we'd actually taken a brilliant action shot! The main 'star' and 'domestic' photos, with their captions, were a great success, graphically illustrating the concept of the book. With the 'Domestic Glossary'; these items were to be the most frequently laughed about, and quoted, over the years.

The book was launched in spring '77, the main event being a party at the International Sporting Club in London. That sounds grand till I add the occasion was used for several books at once, all different subjects, in a multi-purpose publicity bash which soon degenerated into a booze-up.

We got fair reviews in most of the regional papers but attempts to get through to the nationals failed, most saying it was not their policy to review sports books. The best publicity item was provided by John Hughes who played for the Club in the early '60's. He was a freelance sports reporter in the Southampton area, and agreed to send up a television crew to film a short sequence for one of the news programmes. We did this in Stanmer Park one morning, with players and wives making up a 'crowd of spectators'. Some shots were taken of a typical 'domestic' walking out to bat and taking guard, and then I was interviewed by John.

The film was edited into a three minute clip and shown on the southern region of the B.B.C. Nationwide programme at six-fifteen on a certain Tuesday. Before the age of the video recorder, and due to a foul up in our arrangements to see the programme, (not available in the Crowborough area), we missed it. Hence I can't say if it was any good or not!

By the end of the '78 season the dust had settled on the book venture and clearly, 'The Domestic Cricketer' was a failure in commercial terms. 5,000 copies in soft-back form had been printed and only half had been sold at the cover price of £1-65p. The rest were remaindered, with the result that 'sightings' in obscure and remote bookshops have been regularly reported back to me over the years.

One of the last such 'sightings' was the Hull University Students Union 1991 Christmas jumble sale, when a copy in mint condition was bought by a friend of my daughter for 10p.

But a year later saw the most poignant sighting, when my Dad had died, and Carol and my mother called at the Funeral Director's to make the arrangements. Ushered into the flower decked parlour, they were asked to wait a few minutes before seeing the Director. They leafed through various books on a table including, 'The Code of Practice of the National Association of Funeral Directors', 'Funeral Services', 'Facing Bereavement', a catalogue of Memorials and, incredibly – 'The Domestic Cricketer'!

Later, I asked the Director why he kept my book in his parlour, as it didn't seem suitable material. He said; 'Well, it does cheer them up...' adding after careful thought, '...sometimes.'

I personally sold over 700 copies, most of which were signed, so the standing joke over the years has become, the unsigned books are worth far more than the signed ones. And if they're well thumbed having been actually read, then they're extremely rare – possibly worth more than the cover price!

With regard to the serious criticism of the book, I got the impression that those who'd actually played at the lowest level, appreciated and were amused by the idea, readily identifying players in their own clubs as 'stars' or 'domestics'. For those without much knowledge of the game, or playing in a higher standard, it probably seemed too much of a private joke, and a few press reviews were fairly dismissive.

There was however, one bonus in the 'establishment' aspect of the affair which I mention with genuine pride. With no chance of an entry in Wisden on cricketing merit, writing the book allowed me to creep in through the back door. All cricket books usually get a review in Wisden, and in the 1978 edition John Arlott wrote:

'The Domestic Cricketer is built up of all the jokes that beer-cricketers (this reviewer in his day included) have been telling for years; but Mr. Redbourn is the first ever to have them printed. He has, though, set Noel Bennett between book covers as the strategist who, at Christmas, sent in the other side to bat when he observed frozen worm-casts on the length spot.'

It's nice to be first in something, but I wasn't too happy about being classified as a beer-cricketer. Nevertheless, it had all been a lot of fun, though no fortune, and I did receive a few congratulatory letters, treasured to this day.

When St. James's started fielding a Saturday 2nd XI in '77, I was the obvious candidate to take on the captaincy. The side consisted of six or seven colts from fourteen to seventeen, plus a sprinkling of 'golden oldies' no longer mobile enough for the first team. Initially, I was concerned that I'd had no previous experience and had never studied the art of captaincy, but subsequent events rendered my fears redundant.

After three weeks in charge, I altered my approach to each match to that of, 'yet another day in the office'. Getting the side together during the week was hard enough, with complex arrangements necessary to transport the lads to the ground. But that was nothing to what a typical Stanmer home match would involve on the day.

It would start by collecting a couple of lads en route, then when we'd arrived, first ask was to see if we'd got XI, if not, who was missing and why. Then it was helping the tea lady get stuff up to shed, meeting opposition skipper, agreeing intervals, tossing up, getting Club kit in place, rounding up the team and persuading them to get changed.

Next, it was persuading several unwilling players to take out the scoreboard and chairs, put up the sightscreen, and stick in the boundary flags. Then it was providing scorebook and pencil and forcing someone to do the scoring, drawing up batting order, cajoling a senior player to umpire if we were batting, and then change myself.

All that was before the match started! There wasn't much respite on the field either, some of the lads had never been taught fielding positions, so I had to give instructions like: 'Go and stand just inside the boundary on a line between the stumps and the centre of the pond'.

Then again, the youngsters lacked discipline and concentration, so they'd remain static at the end of an over, or if the field changed for left and right-handed batsmen. Worse still, some lads would simply

Stanmer Park on a typical matchday
SC

drift around aimlessly, and I'd suddenly find we'd got three third men. The 'golden oldies' were not much easier to handle either. If the game reached a critical phase, they'd revert to their hey-days and start ordering fielding and bowling changes, so no-one had the faintest idea what was going on, or who was in charge.

I liked to rely on the experienced bowlers to do their stuff and restrict the run rate, when we were fielding first, but even that could end in tears. Peter Gaskell had been a top class medium pacer, and could still tie up most first team batsmen if he put his mind to it. Bringing him back one day, to slow things down, he proceeded to toss up experimental leg-breaks, and three balls passed before I realised what was going on. Furious, I ordered him to bowl properly, but he persisted, so I had to take him off at the end of the over, when the opposition had helped themselves to sixteen.

After the game the work went on, with collecting match fees, clearing up and putting away. Good management theory suggests I should have delegated more, but I reckoned in the long run, it was easier to do it myself. There were some enjoyable moments, but on the whole I found the job exhausting, and was happy to hand over to someone else after two seasons.

By the end of the '70's, I found my role as a 'domestic' and Club official more arduous than enjoyable. As Fixture Secretary I was responsible for arranging the various venues we were forced to use, in order to fulfil our home League obligations. At the same time I tried to make a contribution in the search for our own ground, which involved years of frustration before the first glimmer of success.

But also, my enjoyment of playing in Stanmer Park diminished over the years. The often splendid scene was spoilt when the elm tree overhanging the pond, had to be cut down. Then it started to be promoted as a tourist attraction, buses and coaches would wind up the drive across the front of the House, then park for a time to let the passengers stroll around. With foreign visitors and others uninterested in cricket, they would wander across the outfield, in front of the sightscreens, sometimes near the square, oblivious to the game going on and the dangers of being hit by the ball.

One German visitor I remember, sporting the latest high-tech camera, was so keen to get a close-up of the batsman hitting the ball, he crept up to a position not much deeper than silly mid-off, before we held up play. We spoke no common language and he saw no reason to move, so we ended up having to shoo him away like an obstinate pigeon. Then again, some of the British trippers took the political stance that they were entitled to walk anywhere in a public park, putting priority in exercising their rights above the risk of injury.

At the start of the '80's, I became more involved in the search for the Club's new ground. Initially pessimistic we'd ever get there, with the cost of land and pavilion, but I tried to contribute what I could. All my generation of players, were not only fed up with trailing around the various Brighton and Hove Parks, but desperately keen to ensure the Club's survival, and finish our playing days on our own ground.

When we finally obtained the piece of meadow off the Keymer Road near Ditchling, a sense of relief was quickly followed by determination, to turn it into a cricket ground as soon as humanly possible. As Fixture Secretary through the previous decade, I'd experienced the problems of the wilderness more directly than others. I threw myself into the task with frenetic zeal, determined to make sure I did as much, or more, than anyone else.

With Ian Heath pushing through the construction of the pavilion, I led the task of clearing and levelling the outfield, plus installing an artificial wicket. It was a time of tremendous team spirit and excitement, as we strived in an amateurish way, without proper equipment or sufficient funds, to get the ground into playable shape. The opening match on Sunday 20th June 1982 against Ditchling, was undoubtedly the most exciting and satisfying day of my club cricket career. At last we were in charge of our own affairs, securing the Club's immediate future, with the potential to develop a top class club cricket ground.

Apart from sheer exhilaration, my lasting memories were of a perfect summer day, temperature in the mid-seventies, with slight breeze, deep blue sky, and the occasional scudding cloud. With a rare perfect day for cricket, it almost seemed the Almighty had given a nod of approval for our efforts. No matter the outfield, almost bare of grass, had set hard, the ruts and ledges left by the road roller making normal fielding impossible. Piles of builders rubble were scattered around and, inside the pavilion, furniture and fixtures in the bar and kitchen were in a very rough and ready state.

With champagne before a mid-day start, we played an hour till a salad lunch was conjured up by our womenfolk from the rudimentary facilities. Then a couple of hours before tea, and a final session before we enthusiastically christened the bar from seven o'clock onwards.

In the game itself St. James's batted first and I was given the honour of opening, and facing first ball. As a pessimist I was certain it would shoot along the mat, but the bowler served up a wide full toss to avoid getting me out, and from that combination I managed to top edge the ball down to third man for two. So, I'd scored the first runs on our new ground, and the rest of the day passed in a blur of joy and relief, as we celebrated the most important event since the Club's formation in 1898.

Because I'd organised the matting wicket, and in the absence of volunteers, I effectively became the Club's groundsman, with no knowledge of the skills involved. For the first years the main tasks were repairing damage to the matting, mowing the outfield, and hiring a road roller occasionally, to try and knock down the bumps and ledges.

I enjoyed sitting on the ancient Ransome Triple we'd bought for a song, finding chugging round the field most relaxing, even therapeutic, after a hectic day's work in the office. With a few cronies, we also arranged a work party on Sunday mornings in the winter, to tackle odd jobs on ground and pavilion.

At the end of the '84 season, a problem arose with the Colts section, as there was no-one available to manage the Under-16 side for the following year. I agreed to take on the job, anxious to do my bit in that direction, and encourage my son Mark to play the game.

With matches played mid-week starting at six o'clock, organising transport alone was a complex task, before getting round to the cricket. Most of the lads were from State schools and had received little, if any, coaching, yet their enthusiasm to get involved in competitive sport was infectious.

They integrated quickly into a team and clearly relished an exciting, well contested match. Yet they knew little of the laws, history or techniques of the game, and the task of coaching the youngsters appeared quite daunting, requiring a major team effort to be successful, which at the time we were unable to provide.

With League cricket dominating Saturday fixtures by the mid-'80's, I realised I was going through the motions without much enjoyment. Most of my contemporaries had retired or moved away from the area, and the rapport with the younger generation was not the same. More importantly, games that used to be high spirited, enjoyable affairs, had become tense, aggressive contests, leaving little room for the amateurish, convivial and humorous aspects.

This single-minded drive to win, also meant the cherished traditions of the club game could be ignored, or trampled on. The low point of my disillusionment came in a 2nd XI League match one Saturday. A slip fielder ricked his back going for a catch, and was obviously in severe pain as he was helped off. The Opposition, having initially volunteered a sub, didn't send one out, so we played the last forty minutes with ten men. I was seething when I later heard the 'explanation' from their skipper:

'I couldn't risk sending out a sub; he might've taken a couple of catches and cost us the match.'

The task of Fixture Secretary was not a great time consumer, but I'd found it could never be put down, needing letters to be sent and phone calls made, throughout the year. After years of trying, when I went to St. James's A.G.M in February '87, I'd almost given up hope of ever finding someone else to take over the job.

When asked if I was prepared to stand for office, I made my ritual speech; many errors had crept in, standards were slipping, there was a crying need for fresh blood and new ideas, and so on. Normally no-one listened, and I'd have been re-elected unanimously, with much chat about the need for continuity. On this occasion a newish chap put his hand up and said he was prepared to take over. Jaws dropped and heads swivelled in amazement, and my 19 years in office ended at a stroke.

At the beginning of the '90's, the St. James's and Montefiore Clubs merged, making a host of extra players available. It seemed an appropriate time to move my cricket kit from the wardrobe to the attic, though old club cricketers never retire, they simply fade away.

I advised the Team Secretary I didn't want regular selection, but would be, 'available if required'. This resulted in a few last minute summonses, and I made up numbers on condition I could choose where I fielded, and bat at number 11.

Two years later I amended my instructions to: 'available only if absolutely desperate'.

Thus ended the playing part of my love affair with the greatest game. It was time to observe events from the other side of the boundary rope, usually, in my case, only a step or two away.

CHAPTER 3

THE ALDERMAN

I'll readily admit that my fascination and affection for all things to do with the Brighton Council XI is irrational, and even obsessional. As explanation, I would argue my main playing involvement was when I was new to club cricket, and I'd stumbled across a humorous situation the like of which I'd never seen – or realised could exist – before.

Source of the humour, and focus of all Council XI activities at that time, was a remarkable character, Alderman Percy Friend-James, known throughout the local cricket fraternity as 'the Alderman'. The continuing existence of Council XI cricket was almost entirely for his benefit, everyone else involved being less than enthusiastic.

His personality and the way he dominated affairs were most amusing, as well as the antics on the field. And added to this, was the background of the cut and thrust of local party politics, spiced up with a whiff of social class.

It's impossible to believe such matches could take place in today's world; for a start, we don't make bluff, cricket-crazed ex-Army officers like the Alderman any more. The games had little cricketing merit, often hopelessly one-sided contests, and there was no point in anyone seriously trying to win. And they could never have taken place in modern times, as the whole exercise would've been axed as a waste of rate-payer's money.

To get the full perspective, I've done some basic research into the history of the Brighton Council XI, as background to my experiences over a few seasons. I've taken every opportunity to quiz my cricket pals for fresh anecdotes, and even recently the odd 'Aldermanic nugget' has come to light. I'd have liked to have tracked down scorebooks or written material to add credibility, but all has long since disappeared.

The origins of the Council XI go back into the nineteenth century at least. There's a marvellous sepia photograph of bewhiskered teams titled: 'The first cricket match between the Brighton Town Council and Guardians of the Poor'. This early 'golden age' contest took place at the Dripping Pan in Lewes in 1864.

Perusing through press cuttings in the Braybon family scrapbooks, it's clear a full fixture list of Council XI matches were in operation well before the First World War. Home games were in Preston Park, and it seems most weeks there was a close fought match against Hove, Shoreham, Lewes, or other local Council side. With T.J.Braybon, a leading player of St Mary's C.C., one of the driving forces behind the Brighton XI, it appears the majority of each team were councillors who were also regular club cricketers.

Over the years the proportion of proper cricketing councillors fell, until by the '30's perhaps only three or four had any real club experience, and they were often soldiering on in middle-age. But with matches always taking place in mid-week, it was usually possible to pick up some regular cricketers – ringers in fact – to boost the playing strength.

In 1931 Sir William Dupree, Chairman of the Portsmouth and Brighton United Breweries, donated a trophy for an annual contest between Portsmouth and Brighton Council XI's. The magnificent, ornate gold and onyx creation, currently insured for thousands of pounds, immediately assumed greater importance than the cricket itself, but it did provide a lasting incentive for people to get things organised.

The rules of the competition were for two all-day mid-week games per season, alternating between the two towns and, most importantly, all the players had to be *bona fide* councillors.

This new contest not only gave a shot in the arm for Council cricket but, because of the 'councillors only' rule, meant the majority of players were bound to be non-cricketers. Thus it rapidly evolved into a prime social, rather than sporting, event, with each town vying to outdo the other in the hospitality stakes.

Usual match format was for the teams to meet for cocktails, before a nominal mid-day start and a gentle hour's play. Then, a substantial three course lunch in the Mayor's Parlour, liberally washed down with the full range of wines and shorts, concluded by a short welcoming speech from the host Mayor. Play then re-commenced between two thirty and three for the long afternoon session, with tea taken by four thirty, depending on catering arrangements.

Tables seating four, with parasols and white table linen, were set for all players, wives and officials, and another superb spread consumed. The end of this repast was signalled by the Captain of the visiting XI, who stood up and thanked all and sundry for the hospitality received, replied to any lunchtime comments by the host Mayor, and expressed confidence the last session would be as enjoyable as the first two.

Then into the last hour and a bit, just enough time to give everyone a chance to build up a thirst for the post match drinks session, but before this got under way, there would be a brief ceremony for the winners of the Dupree Trophy. For security reasons, the Cup was kept locked in the boot of the Mayor's car, watched over zealously by the chauffeur, and only taken out at the last minute.

In the last session, drinks were readily available from the fully stocked and staffed bar, specially set up at the ground. Necessarily brief, drinks would be downed swiftly, even desperately, as a coach would be waiting at eight o'clock to take the visitors home.

Within a few years the Trophy matches became the focus of Council XI cricket, with its reputation as a glorious day out not to be missed, growing, as the relevance of the cricket diminished. Though the few cricket playing councillors would be picked automatically, there was a deal of politicking and horse trading, to grab the remaining places.

It was always expected the Mayor of each town would play in the matches, and official engagements were arranged accordingly. And attempts were made, sometimes with disastrous results, to stage manage a starring role for them on the field.

When Percy Friend-James became Mayor of Brighton in the '40's he was nearly fifty, and the Trophy matches were probably his first venture onto a cricket field. Though he'd played rugger and tennis to a good amateur standard, his belated experiences fostered a love affair with his image of cricket, which was to last for the rest of his life.

From my observations, surprisingly, he'd never made any serious attempt to study the Laws, history or techniques of the game, being satisfied with his own credentials on the basis that he, 'had a good eye and was as strong as an ox'. But to be fair, he was humble enough to book coaching lessons in the indoor nets with John Langridge, and it would be nice to say they made a significant improvement to his game.

Though there were a few cricket playing councillors at that time, notably Alderman Sam Davey, a founder member of St. James's, enthusiasm for matches other than the Dupree Trophy was waning, and it was rare for new councillors to show interest in the game.

Over the years matches descended into farce, with unfit middle-aged non-cricketers fooling about on the field, while supposedly engaged in a proper contest. Various myths survive, of players trying to take catches by letting the ball drop into their shirtfronts held outstretched. Of a councillor who became proficient at stopping the ball with his boot, then, too portly to bend, kick it to a colleague to make the return. And it was certainly true that one councillor suffered a mild heart attack going for a risky third run, and was taken to hospital by ambulance!

Left to its natural course, the Council XI fixture list would have quietly faded away by the '60's, leaving the two Trophy matches as mainly social events. But the Alderman had other ideas; by that time he'd bought a full set of kit including wicket-keeping gloves, and considered himself to be a regular club cricketer.

He made himself available to Burgess Hill and other local sides, always making it clear they could expect a generous donation to club funds, a factor which concentrated the selector's minds. Above all, by wielding his undoubted political clout as the senior councillor, he effectively took control of the Brighton Council XI, as organiser and captain, and ran things as his personal fiefdom.

With no regular cricket playing councillors left, the Alderman would call in political favours from all parties, to get colleagues to turn out and form the nucleus of a team. To make up the XI, he would then turn to Frank Osborne or Ken Connatty, prominent local cricketers, to find fill-ins from the Council professional staff.

It became routine on a Tuesday morning for the Alderman to phone Ken and state, 'I need five for this afternoon, Connatty!', and leave him to get on with it. With access to a workforce of several hundred, including regular club players, Ken was usually able to drum up an

XI, though not without protest from Heads of Department, annoyed at losing key personnel at short notice.

When I first played in '62, the Council XI had two or three regular middle aged councillors, plus the odd newcomer who, having had his arm twisted, usually decided one game was enough. Politically, the councillors were evenly divided between the ruling Tories and Labour opposition, Liberals still being over the horizon.

I never understood why the Labour councillors bothered to play, unless it had something to do with expenses or teas, and that was a subject never openly discussed. Before the days of the 'Red Rose', they made little effort to socialise (no pun intended) and took a schoolboy delight in spilling the odd four letter word, to enliven the genteel small talk.

With the rest of the XI made up with good club cricketers, including the odd 'star' player, a full range of abilities were on display. The situation had been reached, whereby the Council matches were arranged for the benefit of a few non-cricketers, with good, regular club players filling in to make up the team. This appetising arrangement stood the normal concept of friendly club cricket on its head, and delivered all sorts of humorous goodies.

My first match as a fill-in, was a home fixture at Stanmer Park. When I arrived in front of the House, it was immediately clear the Alderman dominated affairs: as captain, respected former Mayor, grandee of the local Tory party, and by far the most experienced cricketer of the playing councillors. Also, as the cast assembled, it was clear that everyone accepted the Alderman was in charge.

He'd arrived in an elderly Rover, tipping the waiting Groundsman to take his kit, in a battered brown suitcase, up to the dressing room. He was partly changed, wearing white flannels, brown shoes, open necked and unbuttoned shirt, and a floppy panama hat. I never saw him wearing a sweater, something I understand he considered a sign of weakness.

A powerfully built man with a paunch, he had unruly white hair and walrus moustache, and walked with a slow, shuffling gait. By then in his early sixties, the Alderman had a well established routine, greeting first fellow councillors in order of party and seniority, followed by a brief acknowledgement of the fill-ins.

To be fair, after a few games he remembered surnames, but only a favoured few were granted Christian name terms, and then only if they'd done something outstanding. In response the cast was suitably deferential, calling him 'Sir' or 'Colonel', though the odd senior Tory councillor was bold enough to call him 'Percy'.

Another characteristic soon became apparent; the Alderman had no sense of humour, requiring all cricketing matters to be taken seriously. In some ways, this aspect was the most important of the many features which made up the humorous cocktail. If he'd have laughed at the shenanigans on and off the field as we did, the whole exercise would've become a pointless farce. But no-one dared to chuckle within earshot, as the joke wouldn't have been understood, and he'd probably have been most offended.

For mid-week matches Stanmer Park would be deserted, apart from the players, officials and a few flowery-hatted wives, perhaps persuaded to attend by the prospect of a lavish tea. Before this major event, about ninety minutes play took place, start time being more or less when everyone was ready.

Tea was taken on the lawn to the east of the House, with full paraphernalia unloaded and set out from a large van, which arrived with staff around three o'clock. Of no set duration, the length of the interval was governed by the speeches, though a sense of urgency crept in if the Council XI were due to bat. When someone judged it appropriate, the teams were hushed to a respectful silence, and the Alderman would stand to welcome all and sundry, hoping the second half would be as enjoyable as the first. In reply, the opposing skipper would effusively thank the Alderman for the invitation and hospitality, and drop heavy hints about a repeat fixture the next year.

Close of play was usually seven fifteen, depending on the Alderman's evening engagements, when a bar was set up with free drinks for everyone. With the Alderman a teetotaller, and the other councillors usually just staying for a quick one, the coast was then clear for the hard drinking, regular cricketers.

This dream situation lasted until we went a bit mad one day, polishing off 126 bottles of assorted beers. We would have gone through the lot, but were stopped by the barman shutting up shop, complaining he'd already done enough overtime that week. After that, someone in authority took a cool look at the expense account, and that was that.

In some ways the whole set-up was like a poor man's country house match, with the Alderman squire of the manor, and the rest in supporting roles.

On a Tuesday in May, Derek Pickering and I played our first match for the Alderman, not knowing what to expect though we'd heard rumours. We were in the field and a glance at the opposition openers showed they were overweight and well past their prime.

The Alderman had been tipped off that one of the fill-ins was a star bowler, so he put him on from the bottom end, while he took up his customary wicket-keeping position, about ten yards behind the stumps. As far as the field placings were concerned he took advice from his professional staff, or left everyone to their own devices, though his councillor friends tended to congregate in the slips.

Obviously an unequal contest from the first ball, the batsman groping forward seconds late, the Alderman getting his bulk in line for the stop. This action repeated itself three times, but on the fourth ball the batsman made contact, sending the ball gently into the covers. Delighted with this success, both batsmen set off at a gentle trot down the pitch, assuming an easy run was there for the taking.

At that time, my pal Derek was at the height of his powers as a cover fielder, his pick up and throw as quick as anyone around. He went through his well oiled routine, swooping on the ball 'with pantherine grace', whipping in his return from close to the ground. I can still see now, the ball flashing inches over the stumps, at the precise moment the batsmen crossed in mid wicket.

Having remained static behind the stumps, the Alderman swivelled slowly round to follow the path of the ball, with an expression of amazed distain. It made its way to the boundary by the pond swiftly and unhindered, with a fielder toddling across to find it in the long grass. Still surprised by this turn of events, the Alderman tetchily instructed first slip to take all future returns to the wicket.

Over the weeks, study of the Alderman's wicket-keeping technique revealed he stayed the same distance behind the stumps regardless of the bowler's pace and, unable to crouch in orthodox fashion, would just bend from the waist with gloves in front of knees. With reactions slowed by age, he took some fearful blows from the odd quicker bowler, but would never show, or admit to, any pain.

To be fair, by getting behind the line, he didn't concede that many byes as the ball would bounce off body or gloves. Usually positioned six yards behind the stumps, with a slow bowler his one ploy was to keep a sharp eye on the batsman and, if he spotted him moving out of the crease for any reason including gardening, would creep surreptitiously up to the stumps.

Another amusing aspect of the Alderman's 'keeping, was his method of returning the ball to the bowler. He'd once asked why other 'keepers returned the ball via the slips, and the reason for this was duly explained. He immediately adopted the technique, but with one vital difference. Instead of catching the ball before lobbing to a waiting fielder, he simply deflected it without warning, off his gloves and vaguely into the slip area.

Thus on more than one occasion, I saw the ball hurtle into the crotch of an unsuspecting councillor, as he stood hands on hips, contentedly drinking in the pleasant summer scene. Then in one incident there was astonishment all round, as the Alderman sent the ball racing through gulley to the third man boundary, when he over-did his angle of deflection.

As captain, the Alderman ran the show on the field with some basic rules. A bowler would be put on, regular performer or not, for four overs irrespective of performance or results. When taken off the reason given was either, if successful, 'to give someone else a chance', or if unsuccessful, 'to let someone else have a go'.

John Moore, for many years St. James's opening batsman, recalls a game he played when the Alderman had been tipped off that John was a star player. Never normally a bowler, he was surprised to be thrown the ball as the Council XI went out to field, with the instruction to open the bowling. When he politely pointed out he didn't bowl, he got short shrift from the Alderman who gruffly told him, 'Call yourself a cricketer! Get on with it.'

Politics crept into the task of drawing up the batting order:

councillors first in order of party and seniority, followed by fill-ins whose names the Alderman could remember, followed by the rest. But he was keen to win, and if persuaded a star guest could get quick runs, would adjust the order accordingly.

Off the field the Alderman kept one or two tricks up his sleeve. If he won the toss he always batted first, having an understanding with the Council umpire that he'd produce an old ball, saving the new one till after tea. Likewise, there was a useful arrangement with the caterer, who'd stroll around the boundary from four o'clock onwards. If it suited the Alderman to take an early tea, he'd give a signal and the chap would hurry onto the field, holding up play to announce tea was ready.

It was well known that the Alderman disapproved of the opposition batting on after tea; he liked the game divided into halves, especially if the timing of the interval was variable.

A lovely incident on this theme was a match against a Brighton Teachers XI captained by Derek Stenton, a regular Rottingdean player. On a wet wicket at Stanmer, the Teachers batted first and struggled to make headway against two 'star' fill-in bowlers. With late start and early tea, they were only 90 for 4 at the interval, and an embarrassed and apologetic Stenton approached the Alderman to say:

'I'm dreadfully sorry sir, but with the late start and the difficult wicket, I'm afraid I've got no option but to bat on.'

Affronted, the Alderman's immediate reply brooked no further discussion:

'You can't! And in any case, you've had the best of the wicket.'

The Council XI then knocked off the runs comfortably on a drying track after tea, and everything was wrapped up soon after six o'clock.

One of the classic matches of my season with the Council XI, with two of the most farcical incidents I've ever seen on a cricket field, was against a side put together by Brighton Transport Department. Not surprisingly they arrived in a double-decker, parked in front of Stanmer House, disgorging a stream of high spirited young men, who gambolled about like lambs let out in the spring sunshine. In seconds one could deduce that most had never played before, and we were going to have to work hard to make a game of it.

Rushing eagerly up to the changing room, clutching plimsolls, sweaters and white shirts, perhaps one or two had risen to a brown carrier bag. I focussed on one chap, early thirties, who looked much like Reg Varney of 'On the Buses' fame, and also had his infectious, wild-eyed exuberance.

The Transport XI batted first and 'Reg' came out to open, brimming with excitement at probably his first venture onto a cricket field. To the first ball he executed a horrendous, cross batted heave, eyes firmly shut, but miraculously made perfect contact, sending it soaring towards cowshot corner. Elated, he raced off down the wicket, waving bat aloft, making no call to his partner who was dithering about at the other end.

Going full tilt on a greasy surface wearing plimsolls, 'Reg' learnt his first lesson when he tried to turn on a sixpence, and ended up in a muddied heap three yards past the stumps. With shrieks of encouragement from the boundary, the non-striker was finally about to run, when he switched priority to attend to the winded 'Reg'.

Our all action hero however, had no such hesitations and looking for the second, bounced up and set off full pelt for the other end. Had he run his bat along the ground he'd have made the crease easily, but glancing towards the thrower, saw the ball hurtling through the air on its way to the stumps. Panicking, he made a sprawling, belly flop dive, skidded for some distance, and came to a halt with bat just short of the crease. With commendable determination, he then levered himself forward a few inches to make his ground and beat the throw.

The excitement of this dramatic start was not yet over; the scorers came onto the field, in heated dispute as to how many runs were made. It was definitely two according to the Transport man, but the Council scorer knew otherwise. In effect, the Alderman then appointed himself match referee and solemnly awarded one run.

Reg survived for another couple of overs, before being bowled by the first straight ball he received. Events continued in that style, but went downhill when the Alderman invited Cllr Denis Hobden to bowl the customary four overs from the Church end. Though a non-cricketer, the Councillor was passably kitted out, except for footwear where he hadn't managed an alternative to his brown, Chelsea suede boots.

I don't know what was in the Councillor's mind when he got the ball, but he marched to the wicket and paced out a fifteen yard run-up with an air of confidence and authority. He then tried to make a mark, but the thick crepe soles of his boots made no impression on the surface, greasy on top but hard underneath.

As we watched fascinated, he gave that up and ran in to a suitably alarmed and apprehensive batsman. But as he neared the wicket he slowed appreciably, till standing almost still between the creases. From there he launched a high altitude lob, to which the batsman, on a par cricketwise, took an energetic cross batted swish, failing to disturb the ball as it bobbled gently past the stumps. This action was repeated for the next three deliveries, as the Councillor sought to pitch nearer the target, and the batsman flailed strenuously to make contact.

Then on the fifth ball, as if determined to commit suicide, the batsman lurched yards down the track before executing his swish with such force, he swung himself off his feet, ending up on his back, head towards the stumps. The ball meanwhile, bounced unhindered along the side of his body and trickled up to tap off stump, with just sufficient force to dislodge a bail.

In other circumstances, a regular cricketer would have laughed openly, but that was unacceptable in Council matches. Fielding in the deep I chuckled away un-noticed, but couldn't contain my mirth on this occasion, when the Alderman congratulated his bowler with:

'Well bowled Denis; just the breakthrough we needed!'

Fielding after tea, 'Reg' was posted to mid-on and crouched there menacingly for the opening over. When the batsman decided to take a look at the bowling, 'Reg' interpreted this as a sign of weakness, and crept in ever closer. By the last ball, with 'Reg' almost at silly mid on, our man had got his bearings, and whipped the ball off his toes towards 'Reg' at some speed.

A sharp catch for a good fielder, 'Reg' had no idea what to do, so self preservation took over. He shot his legs forward, clamped hands over face and sat down heavily, allowing the ball to streak across the top of his head. He'd felt the ball parting his hair and, as it dawned on him how close he'd come to a nasty injury, his demeanour changed.

His shoulders slumped and colour drained from his face as he trudged back to deep mid-on, from where he showed no interest in the rest of the game. In a few hours he'd moved from a naive, enthusiastic novice, to an embittered and disgruntled, former player.

A rich source of humour in the Council matches was the 'one for the off' tradition, something the Alderman regarded as an essential part of the game. Most of the regulars on the circuit knew this, and willingly tossed up a few friendly ones to a new batsman, especially if he was a councillor, or the Alderman himself.

Indeed, it became so well established it was considered a cardinal sin to get a batsman out first ball, and bowlers became distinctly nervous, even paranoid, about this. But accidents did happen, and I relate some of the the best ones below.

David Laing was only fourteen, making his debut in Council cricket, when he filled in for the Gentlemen of the Press against the Council XI at Stanmer Park. The Press wanted to give the young lad a chance, so he kept wicket and was doing a grand job till the Alderman came in to bat. With Jim Pegg lobbing up his ultra slow leg breaks at the time, there seemed no need to make special arrangements for the first ball, but David hadn't been briefed on proceedure.

Taking guard in his usual cursory manner, the Alderman faced up and Jim Pegg pitched the ball well outside off stump to avoid any mishap. The Alderman shuffled two foot down the pitch, swished across to leg, and missed. Young David, seeing him well out of his ground, efficiently swept off the bails, appealing triumphantly. This was immediately answered with a firm, 'Not out'.

Amazed, but not to be beaten, David noticed the Alderman was still standing out of his ground. Fully conversant with the Laws, he pulled a stump up with ball in glove, and appealed again. When this was again swiftly turned down he was stunned, but could only seethe with indignation at the injustice.

At the end of the over, the square leg umpire beckoned sternly to the young lad, and when towering over him, spelt out the facts of Council cricket life in words of one syllable:

'Look son; you don't even think about getting the Alderman out, till he's got a few runs on the board'.

Another super incident on this subject, was when the Mayor of that year, Alderman Button, was persuaded to play for the Council XI against the R.A.F. Association. I suspect the Mayor only turned out reluctantly in the call of duty, and that he'd never played cricket before.

Mindful of the dignity of his office, the Mayor was fully kitted out and, straight backed and over six foot, he cut an impressive figure. When the Alderman won the toss he naturally elected to bat, and invited the Mayor to open the innings, against an opposition who thought it was a normal game of cricket.

Going out to open, I sensed the Mayor wasn't enjoying this venture into the unknown, with the prospect of facing first ball. To make matters worse, it was to be bowled by the R.A.F.A.'s star quickie, a man who regarded anyone wearing pads with some contempt. Having fiddled about taking guard, no-one had told the Mayor about making a mark, so he just crouched into a reasonable stance and peered hopefully down the wicket.

The first ball was certainly swift, swinging away and taken waist high by the 'keeper standing well back. Whether he saw the ball or not, the Mayor remained frozen in position. The second ball was an action replay, though closer to the stumps, but the third was smack on target and thudded into the Mayor's pads. A confident appeal by the bowler was instantly turned down by the Council umpire, as the Mayor, grimacing with pain, hobbled around trying to maintain some dignity. By this time there were frantic signals and hoarse whispers from the boundary, which some of the visiting side were taking on board, but too late for the fourth delivery. This demolished the Mayor's stumps as he remained static, squinting down the track, his face still contorted with pain.

From the bowler's viewpoint, that was the end of the argument, and he started his victory dance, expecting to be showered with praise from his colleagues. But the resourceful Council umpire retrieved the situation, with probably the latest ever call of 'No ball!'. After initial tantrums, the incredulous quickie became philosophical, convinced it was his incredible bad luck to have run into the most crooked umpire of all time.

At this point the R.A.F.A. skipper had got the message, and rushed across to have a 'quiet word' with his bowler. Fired up and extremely annoyed, he dismissed his skipper's pleas out of hand. 'Where I come from,' he said, 'there's no quarter asked or given, they don't play mickey mouse cricket, and the only place for a batsman is back in the hutch.'

The skipper withdrew defeated, and we waited helplessly the inevitable calamity of the fifth ball. When this demolished the woodwork again, the Mayor wisely decided to call it a day, and limped off gamely, feigning a smile. He hadn't lifted his bat from the stance position throughout this trauma, and when he reached the boundary there was an embarrassed silence. No-one could think what to say, but the Alderman had no inhibitions and offered a cheery:

'Bad luck Mr Mayor!'

It was a kind sentiment, though somewhat stretching the truth.

My favourite 'one for the off' incident took place at Stanmer in a match against a NALGO XI, all of whom were fully familiar with the niceties of Council cricket. The central character was a Labour councillor who'd been persuaded to turn out, one suspected, much against his better judgement.

I didn't know his name and only saw him play once, but he was a tall, powerfully built man, with black hair, beetle brows and moustache, and taciturn to the point of being speechless. He'd gone to the trouble of procuring some basic kit, and if he'd never played before, he'd tried to pick up a couple of clues, to avoid making too much of a fool of himself.

On a pleasant day, the Council XI batted first, a sprinkling of spectators enjoying the action with the batting side, in deck chairs in front of the House. A couple of wickets fell and the Alderman went in, all the NALGO side concentrating on avoiding his early dismissal, a hazard safely negotiated.

Thus far the match being nicely stage managed, another wicket fell heralding the entrance of the beetle browed Labour Councillor. Though his clothing looked smart, his batting kit only stretched to one pad and one glove, and his journey to the crease didn't inspire confidence, being unsure of which end to aim for.

For this game I was playing for NALGO, keeping wicket in fact, and an old pal of mine Brian Hunter, a useful medium pacer, was bowling at the time. In a good position to watch the action, the Councillor took guard, made a mark, then slumped heavily on his bat waiting the first ball.

Brian had decided to play safe by tossing up an experimental legger, but at the last moment changed his mind about spinning the ball, in case it turned behind the Councillor's legs and bowled him. Unhappily he lost control, the ball sailing high and straight over the bat hitting the top of off stump full toss, with the Councillor unseeing and unmoving.

Mortified, we all studied our toe-caps in silence, while the Councillor seemed unaware as to what had happened. Finally an embarrassed close fielder moved towards him to whisper apologetically:

'I'm dreadfully sorry sir; I'm afraid you're out'.

The Councillor said nothing at this point but, as he walked off, became more enraged as it dawned on him what all his preparations for an afternoon's cricket had amounted to.

At the other end, the Alderman had watched this tragedy unfold, shaking his head in sorrow, perhaps feeling an element of personal responsibility for his colleague's demise. Breaking the still tense silence, he called out as the Councillor neared the boundary:

'Not a very friendly one for first ball; was it Councillor?'

Unable to contain his rage any longer, this question triggered an explosion, and the Councillor bellowed out the unprintable, monosyllabic reply:

'C***!!!'

This foulest of all four lettered words, seemed to echo from the House and surrounding trees, as the whole cast froze in horror at such an unbelievable outrage. Spectators visibly cringed, eyes rivetted again on toe-caps, and a wide path was cleared for the offender.

Had the teas been prepared, no doubt the bone china would have shattered instantly. No one went near, or spoke to, the Councillor after this, and he became a social outcast, not even granted token party political support. It was the most dramatic use of an expletive I can recall, with devastating affect on the genteel and civilised atmosphere of the occasion.

When I've asked players what single aspect they most remembered from their experiences of Council matches, the answer was always the same, playing in appalling weather. The Alderman simply didn't accept that cricket couldn't sensibly be played, let alone enjoyed, in pouring rain and thick mud. Considering the number of times it rains in a typical English summer, it's not surprising there's a number of stories on this theme.

Ken Connatty, who bore the brunt of the organisational side of Council matches, recalls the morning of a match when it had rained all night, and was still pouring hard at mid-day. He thought it polite to phone the Alderman to confirm the game was off, before he advised the players:

'Obviously sir, with the overnight rain and no sign of any let up, I assume this afternoons game is off?'

The Alderman's emphatic reply left no room for discussion:

'These games are always on Connatty; tell the men to bring their gumboots!'

Another time he arrived for a Stanmer match, after two days of unbroken rain, and pulled up in front of the House. The groundsman, in boots and full oilskins, trudged across to the car, shaking his head slowly from side to side. As the Alderman wound down the window, the groundsman sadly advised:

'I'm terribly sorry sir, the pitch is completely waterlogged. I'm afraid the game's off.'

The Alderman's cheery reply, instantly over-ruling him was:

'Oh that's quite alright; we'll manage.'

A lovely incident I saw at Stanmer one day, was in a match that started in pleasant, warm conditions, with blue sky and just the odd cloud. The batting side and spectators, in shirtsleeves, were in deck chairs on the grass in front of the House, with the Alderman nearest to the pitch in customary unbuttoned shirt and floppy hat.

The clouds became more frequent and darker, until a menacing black one could be seen moving towards us from opposite the House. We could all hear the hiss of rain hitting the trees, and without waiting for the umpire's decision, sprinted off to find cover.

The Alderman was distinctly unimpressed by all this, remaining slumped in his chair as people rushed past. Then he made his feelings felt with the caustic comment:

'What're you all made of then; tissue paper?'

The worst conditions I ever played in, for the Council XI or anyone else, was a special fixture against Brighton Rotary Club in September one year, at Withdean Stadium. The ground was soft from earlier rain, more falling steadily on the morning of the match, and with haze and solid low cloud, it looked a typical, depressing mid-winter scene.

With much preparation for the game, a morning cancellation was out of the question, so players gathered in the Sportsman pub at lunchtime, for the formal statement it had been rained off. With no wind or break in the dense cloud cover, no one took much notice when the Alderman splashed out to 'have a look at the wicket' at two thirty.

There were many players new to Council cricket on parade, and they barely stiffled laughter when the Alderman solemnly announced on his return, that he thought things were getting better, and an early tea would be taken with a view to getting under way at four thirty.

Protest was muted by the prospect of tea, assumed to be up to the usual Council standard. This was duly much enjoyed by all and in his speech afterwards, the Alderman casually mentioned conditions were not ideal. But he added, he was confident a match could be played, and would report further after another pitch inspection.

By the time he'd squelched back again from the middle, with no prospect of the rain easing, everyone had become resigned to the fact that a match would be played, and they'd have to stand in the field for a couple of hours getting soaked to the skin.

The fielding side trooped out, gloomily unenthusiastic, wrapped up as best they could against the elements. When the game got under way, bowlers quickly reduced their run-ups to a few paces, and batsmen swung at the ball while rooted to the spot, trying not to swing themselves off their feet.

Highlight of this farce was when a portly middle-aged Rotarian went to the wicket, immaculately clad from head to toe in new cricket kit, bought only the day before. Having swished and missed for an over or

The Alderman leads his men into the fray at Stanmer Park. Two short?

Star

so, he finally made contact, setting off for a run to be met with a firm 'No!' from the other end. Attempting to stop in smooth soled plimsolls, he sat down abruptly in mid wicket and, seeming to accept his likely fate, made no attempt to retrieve the situation.

He turned to watch as the ball was returned to the Alderman, poised over the stumps for the kill. But when it bounced off his gloves three yards to one side, the Rotarian decided it worth making an effort to get back. Scrambling to his feet he accelerated too fast, ending up sliding towards the crease face down, just a few inches short. The Alderman meanwhile, having picked up the ball then dropped it, finally clutched it in glove before sweeping the bails off in triumph.

I remember the expressions of horror and disbelief on his wife's face, as the Rotarian squelched in, looking as if he'd just finished a tough mid-winter game of rugger.

Thankfully the rain eased up towards the end, but the mist closed in; at one point it wasn't possible to see fielders in the deep, from the other side of the field. I don't think I've ever looked forward to a hot shower so much when it was all over, but found out there was only cold; the boilers had been switched off as an economy measure!

I didn't play in the match accepted, by mutual agreement of the regulars, as the ultimate farce in Council cricket, so far as the weather was concerned. It was between the Council XI and the Staff and scheduled for an eleven thirty start at Stanmer.

Having rained continuously for the previous two days, it is actually true that flood alerts were being tackled in the town, and only one person was giving any consideration to a game of cricket. On the morning of the match, it was still raining heavily with rolls and claps of thunder, with the square under water which had nowhere to go.

Because of the sensitive working relationship between councillors and professional staff, all the cast had deemed it wise to assemble at Stanmer House. The groundsman immediately advised that, as the forecast was for yet more rain, the game should be cancelled.

Ignoring this, the Alderman without consulting the opposing skipper, decided an early lunch would be taken with pitch inspection at one o'clock. No-one complained too much because lunch was; salmon steaks washed down with muscadet, sherry trifle, cheese and biscuits, and coffee.

At the appointed hour the Alderman and a few others, splashed out to the middle in conditions that had, if anything, deteriorated. After a cursory glance at the pond of water and ignoring the pleas of everyone else, the Alderman announced the match would start in half an hour, not even bothering to suggest that things were likely to improve.

The Council XI – including the Mayor only turning out in the call of duty – waded out to the middle to field in ridiculous conditions. Most players had trouser bottoms rolled up, bowlers fought to keep a foothold, and immobile batsmen flailed at the ball as it shot along the surface.

After twenty minutes of this farce, and the rain getting heavier, the Mayor decided to communicate his displeasure by leaving the field, to return wearing plastic mac, trousers rolled up to the knees and carrying an umbrella. Resolve strengthened by this demonstration, the rest of the team brought their protests to the point of mutiny, and ten minutes later the Alderman gave way, reluctantly agreeing to abandon the match.

By the mid-sixties the Council XI fixture list had declined, opposition for these mid week games becoming harder to find, and only the Alderman retaining his enthusiasm. Wielding his authority, he managed to retain a few social matches, but it was the two prized Dupree Trophy games that really mattered.

Because of the 'councillors only' rule, for some years there'd been no-one playing for the Brighton side in the Trophy matches, with any real cricketing skill or experience. Then in '66 David Laing, regular opening batsman for Preston Nomads, got himself elected to the Council when at the peak of his cricket career.

This was manna from heaven to the Alderman, who reckoned the newcomer would be able to win matches on his own, and plotted to use him like a secret weapon. David remembers two Dupre matches against Portsmouth, when he was supposed to play the starring role, with mixed results. With his help I've tried to reconstruct them.

The first occasion was the usual all-day affair at Stanmer; the ground set out with all the trimmings on a perfect day for cricket.

The Alderman having won the toss batted first, proudly sending David out to open with Cllr. Baker. A quick glance round the changing room, had already told David he'd have to work hard if the match was to last much beyond the lunch interval. It was not so much the task of scoring himself, but that of protecting the other batsmen.

Taking first strike, David took control by taking a single off the last ball of each over, hitting one or two fours before that. This worked the score up to 35, with no mis-haps and without his partner touching the ball.

Then during an over, Cllr Baker, unable to understand what was going on, called a mid wicket conference and said in effect; 'Can I have a go?' As much the junior councillor David had to agree, so he pushed back the last ball to concede strike. Exact details of what happened next are unclear but, suffice to say, in the next two overs five wickets fell before David managed to snatch back the strike.

He then continued his tactics, taking the total up to 75 when a similar thing happened, three wickets falling in as many overs. This brought in Cllr Theobald who'd played some cricket earlier in his life, knew what David was trying to do, and became a willing accomplice. They grafted away to add 70 for the ninth wicket before Cllr Theobald was out, leaving David to fashion another twenty with the last man.

David had scored 143 not out from a total of 165, but more to the point, had ensured the match lasted till after tea. He can't remember whether Portsmouth reached the target or not, but thanks to him a jolly good time was had by all.

The second Trophy match involved much plotting and scheming, all to no avail. It was at Portsmouth, and for some reason was shortened to an afternoon game with two o'clock start. David had warned the Alderman that because of urgent business in the morning, he'd probably be late, but go straight to the ground when he arrived.

Hospitality for the other players and officials started around twelve thirty, with cocktails in the Mayor's Parlour, before moving into the Dining Room for the usual three course meal. During coffee, the Mayor of Portsmouth stood to welcome his guests and look forward to a sterling contest on the field of play. Meanwhile the Alderman had been keeping a sharp eye on the door, hoping David would burst through to signify his presence.

When the Mayor sat down, the Alderman produced his masterstroke. To everyone's surprise he jumped to his feet, and launched into a speech of thanks, normally reserved for the tea interval. Starting off with the customary pleasantries, he then constructed a filibuster, using his debating skill and long experience.

Not only did he thank individually, just about everyone in the building, but detailed their vital contribution to the day's merriment. He then moved on to a wider canvas, to extol the virtues of municipal co-operation, praise the role of sport in a civilised society, and stress the importance of a healthy mind being supported by a healthy body.

David Laing meanwhile, had reached the ground at two o'clock to find no-one there, so he drove on to the Town Hall. When he entered the Dining Room the Alderman was still in full flow, but relieved to see David's arrival, quickly wrapped up his speech. Everyone then moved off to the ground, the game starting about forty minutes late.

The Alderman won the toss and batted, opening with David and the

Mayor, a middle-aged non-cricketer. David faced first ball which, off the back foot, he pushed hard and straight to mid-wicket, with no thought of a run.

As he watched the fielder pick up the ball, he became aware of the Mayor bearing down on him rapidly, issuing the sharp command:

'Come on move! Or we'll never get any runs.'

As a Council newcomer, somewhat in awe of his much senior colleague, David felt he had no option but to attempt the run. Setting off on the hopeless task, he watched mid wicket swivel and flick the ball underarm, to take out middle stump at the bowlers end. Run out by almost a pitch length David retired to the pavilion, gamely saying it was all his fault.

The mid-wicket fielder, apart from being a generation younger than his colleagues, possessed a full set of kit which fitted properly and clearly knew what he was doing. But he spent most of his time at third man and wasn't brought on to bowl, though most of his team mates got a few overs.

It turned out to be a genuinely close finish, with Portsmouth needing eight to win when the ninth wicket fell, and the 'star' fielder went out to bat as last man. Only three balls were necessary; the first, having glanced around the off side field, he cut backwards of square for four. The second he thumped straight back towards the bowler who, inspite of desperate evasive action, was unable to avoid a painful blow. The third he rocked forward onto his toes and flicked the ball wristily passed square leg for four.

Intrigued by this, David found a chance to quiz the Portsmouth captain during the drinks session later, about why he hadn't used such an obvious 'star' performer. The skipper dismissed the question as if the answer was obvious:

'He's new to the Council, and in any case, he's a member of the Opposition'.

Ken Connatty remembers the last match the Alderman played, in fact only a few weeks before he died. By then it appeared the Alderman had at last recognised the limits of his own strength, and appointed someone else to keep wicket while he stood at mid on.

It was a hot September day at Stanmer Park, in the long established fixture against the crew from H.M.S. Hero. Before the Council XI went out to field, the Alderman took one of his team aside and said with a flourish:

'I want you to keep wicket. You can borrow my gloves – they're the best that money can buy!'

After the Alderman, the Council XI fixture list was reduced to just the two Trophy matches, and these continued to '82 when the Brighton XI cried off, unable to raise a side. Some efforts have been made to revive the contest since then, while the Trophy itself sits collecting dust and increasing in insurance value.

Whatever I've said about the Alderman in this chapter, he was a buffoon in the cricket sense only, and under the bluff, no nonsense exterior, I believe was a kind and generous man.

The Dupre Trophy should at least be suitably inscribed to his memory, and possible wording would be:

'To the Alderman; stout leader, lovable cricket fanatic, fearless wicket-keeper, and greatest all-weather player.'

CHAPTER 4

BRIGHTON BRUNSWICK

Playing a few games for Brighton Brunswick C.C., as a fill-in, was the closest I got to top grade club cricket. The Brunswick are one of the senior and most prestigious Clubs in Sussex, with their origins linked to the County Club. They started playing on the Brunswick lawns on Hove seafront, and then moved on to the new Eaton Road Ground, with Sussex, when it first came into use in 1870. Sharing the same Ground, many Sussex players have turned out for the Brunswick, before or after their first class careers, including seven Test cricketers: E.H.Bowley, P.G.H.Fender, W.A.Humphries, W.L.Murdoch, D.V.Smith, N.I.Thompson and J.Vine.

I can't remember how I got involved with the Brunswick in the early '60's, but somehow my name found it's way into the little black book of 'Ossie' Osborne who, for the whole of my playing time, appeared to run the Brunswick almost single-handedly. A 'doer' with unquenchable enthusiasm for the game, he was Fixture and Team Secretary at the time, when the Club played about twenty mid-week matches a season, with most home games on the County Ground.

'Ossie' built up a list of star players from the leading Sussex club sides to assemble his XI for each match, but he also needed additional names he could call on, to make up numbers, or as last minute fill-ins. On this basis, and my friendship with Peter Beecheno, I played a dozen or so matches, enough to form some lasting impressions.

Firstly, though we hadn't developed the term then, it was a team of stars and fill-ins, but no 'domestics'. For key matches the side would be packed with 'stars', and in lesser games, 'Ossie' usually got enough key players to handle all the expected batting and bowling. This meant that the extras like me, went along for the ride and the chance to rub shoulders with the 'stars'.

Another memory was of the clique of senior players who formed an exclusive drinking school after a match. They drank shorts only, and scotch on the rocks and pink gin, were quaffed at a frantic rate. For someone who'd only just mastered the art of downing pints of shandy, to do the same with shorts was another mountain to climb.

After a number of games as a Brunswick fill-in, I still savour the day I cocked a snook at the 'stars', in a match when I didn't know anyone in the side. It was against Horley, in August '64, and the only time I ever played on the main table of the County Ground at Hove.

It was a mild overcast day when we reluctantly assembled at the Tate Gates, having been dragged out of the 'Cricketer' pub by the skipper. As we trooped up to the players entrance at the back of the Main Stand, it appeared all the other players knew each other, and there was much banter as we climbed the stairs to the players balcony and changing rooms at the top.

Effectively on my own, I was overcome by the sense of history, with ghosts of the past, by the time we reached the top. Three of the stars, Whitehead, Tetley and Smith, dumped their kit in the middle of the floor, and continued their animated discussion oblivious of everyone else. The others milled around while our skipper, Jimmy Barker, strolled out to the middle with his Horley opposite number.

Jimmy was about 50, a tail end batsman only, who captained, managed, and generally organised everything throughout the game. It all seemed a bit much for him at times, plus the fact that most of his instructions and chivvying were totally ignored.

As he returned from the middle, he refused to signal what we were doing, in spite of much encouragement to do so. Eventually, as he reached the balcony to a chorus of, 'What we doing Jimmy?', he announced; 'Gentlemen, we are bat...!'.

Before he could finish, there were whelps of joy from everyone - except the three batting stars - as they rushed back down to the 'Cricketer', to get in a few more pints before two thirty closing time.

Vaguely aware of this from the back of the balcony, I was still engrossed in the fact that the very same studded and splintered floorboards I was standing on, had been trodden by Compton, Hutton, Bradman, Hobbs, Trumper, and W.G. even.

Jimmy Barker then busied himself drawing up his batting order, with just the five of us left in the stand. It's clear now, the three stars had not moved because they knew they'd be changing, either to bat or field. Jimmy politely interrupted their discussion, and nominated them one, two and three, to which they barely nodded in acceptance. Having done the easy bit, he then looked round the balcony to see what was left. Spotting me skulking at the back, he glanced hopefully around, before he approached to ask my name. Writing that down, he took a last despairing look round, peering into every corner, before saying reluctantly: 'Well…er, you better go four.'

We got changed and padded up, and the game started at one thirty sharp. Within half an hour two wickets fell, and I found myself walking, creeping almost, out to bat, only the lack of spectators limiting my self-consciousness. Indeed, apart from the players, scorers and umpires, there was no-one else in the Ground, except a small boy manfully trying to operate the main scoreboard.

Horley were short of pace bowling on the day, so I faced Bill Roper, a slow off-spinner, with a pre-programmed forward push in my first over. About fourth ball I accidentally connected perfectly, and was amazed to watch it race away between cover and extra for four.

The flat, rock hard, billiard table surface highlighted a crucial difference between club and first-class cricket; a soggy Stanmer Park being a sand pit by comparison. I was able to cope with a slow club bowler, but I'm sure anyone appreciably quicker, would have been through me in an over or two.

It was interesting batting for a while with footballer Dave Sexton, later Manager of Manchester United. An elegant, straight bat player, he had time to play his shots, and scored 40 without raising sweat. With confidence growing, I bashed the ball around until I reached 85, when, with the glory of a century beckoning, I hit wicket with a wayward late cut. In eerie silence I departed the scene, glancing about hopefully, that applause might somehow materialise.

Clambering triumphantly up to the players balcony, I expected a warm welcome, with much back slapping all round. To my surprise, I received only a muted 'Well batted', from several players, with the inference; 'Look old boy, we don't mind you having a go while we're down the pub, but you're not supposed to hog all our batting time!'

We scored 282 for 9 declared at tea, after which we bowled Horley out for 140. This part of the game was also memorable in that, as a player, I witnessed at close hand the most brilliant piece of wicket-keeping

I've ever seen. The Brunswick opening bowlers were Peter Hanley and Harry Newton, and it soon became clear they were too much of a handful for the Horley batsmen. Behind the stumps was Terry Gunn the understudy to Sussex and England 'keeper Jim Parks, and someone many thought was a better wicket-keeper as such.

Harry Newton, who also played the odd game for Sussex, was fast at club level, and about medium-fast by first class standards. The situation arose where he was bowling flat out from the south end, with Gunn standing up, and me cowering in the gully. Because he was bowling a bit too short, the pace and bounce meant the Horley batsmen couldn't get near the ball.

Gunn, standing right up on the stumps, positioned his gloves, between waist and head level, as the ball pitched. He would then catch it, without discernible give, and sweep it down to hover by the bails.

I had to steel myself each ball, praying the batsman wouldn't make contact, as it would have come at me like a shell. This would have provided an unwanted, and potentially embarrassing test of my physical courage, diving for cover in that company wouldn't have been appreciated.

The other match to leave a lasting, but painful impression, was at Catford one year, when there'd been heavy rain the preceeding week. Both pitch and outfield looked lush green and, whoever won the toss, Brunswick batted first. Having not had a decent knock previously that season, I was pleased to be told by the skipper, he was giving me a chance up the order at number five.

In no time at all, three of our front line stars were out and, at 23 for 3, the moment of truth had abruptly arrived. The skipper, trying to hide his state of panic, came over to give me a serious pep talk before I went in. I listened respectfully, the gist of his instructions being: defend like mad and don't even think about trying to score runs for at least half an hour.

From the boundary, the bowler I'd be facing had looked pretty innocuous. He was stocky, grey haired, nearer fifty than forty, and off eight paces looked a slow-medium trundler, though from the carnage he'd caused I realised it couldn't be as simple as that. I took guard carefully and, summoning every ounce of concentration and determination, faced up to the first ball.

It came through twice as fast as I'd expected, but was well wide of off stump and swinging further away. Though I wouldn't have been quick enough to make contact anyway, leaving it was the correct option. At least I'd gleaned an idea what he was doing, but my heart sank as I turned to watch the 'keeper take the ball chest high in front of first slip.

The second ball was repeat of the first, but starting on a line nearer to off stump. I only had to think briefly, before allowing it to swing away without playing a stroke.

The third ball was much more difficult. It's initial line was just outside off stump, and I was torn between trying to smother it with a firm forward push, or gamble on it swinging safely away again. Before my brain had resolved the problem, the ball was through, missing the stumps by some nine inches, and veering strongly away towards the slips.

The fourth ball started off on exactly the same line and, with growing confidence, I quickly decided it was safe to let it through again. It was an in-swinger.

As I trudged back to the pavilion, head bowed, I felt more dejected and inadequate than at any other time in my cricket career. I'd been rolled over with ludicrous ease, by someone old enough to be my father, and probably well past his best. I'd failed abjectly to answer the call on the one occasion I'd been asked to make an important contribution to a Brunswick match. And in a wider sense, I'd destroyed any lingering hopes I had, that I might be good enough to play at this level of the game.

Though I did little on the field, my brief association with the Brunswick, at least enabled me to observe at close quarters, some of the best club players in the County. I'd also picked up much gossip about the annual week long tour to Devon, playing strong clubs such as Plymouth, Exeter and Sidmouth. Clearly, there was some fine cricket on the field, mixed in with heavy drinking and, I'm told, other dubious activities.

A typical Tour story was of an all day game against Torquay, when

John Lawson and Derek Grammer emerged from the pavilion, to open the batting. Looking shades of green or white after the night before, they only managed a few yards before being obliged to sprint behind the pavilion to be violently ill. That done, they re-started their entrance and proceeded to score a century each.

With the base established at the Palm Court Hotel Torquay, the Tour became a must for the star players and enthusiasm grew to include serious golf.

I remember listening, open mouthed, to a conversation involving Peter Beecheno, having just returned from a Tour. With relish he described a typical day as: champagne breakfast, a round of golf, the cricket match, drinking in the bar till the early hours, followed by cards till breakfast. 'Indeed…', he said finishing with a flourish, '…we travelled down on Saturday and I didn't go to bed 'till Thursday morning!'

As someone who's always valued my sleep, I made a mental note never to get involved with the Brunswick Tour, by accident or design.

———◦◦◦◦———

Over the years, one escapade in the Brunswick history has been recounted time and time again, by veterans of the post war era. Its become a legendary tale of the days before the breathalyser, when to end up 'legless' was the prime objective, when the lads were out on the town.

I contacted some of the players involved, and was amazed at the detail they could recall of events 35 years ago. With their memories I've pieced together a fairly accurate picture of this episode, which I hope will give the flavour of a bygone age, and the cavalier spirit of the Brunswick.

The match was a mid-week all day affair against Old Redingensians, at the School Ground Reading in July '56. Further afield than most club matches in that era, the fixture was made through Geoff Davis who, at that time, was landlord of the Royal Oak pub in St. James's Street Brighton. A keen and regular Brunswick player, he was also an Old Redingensian, and due to move back to his home town to take a larger pub, the 'Jack of Both Sides'.

The mid-week all day match was arranged as a celebration, but the 'long' journey was made more difficult by petrol rationing in the Suez crisis. A great man for a party, Geoff Davis suggested the Brunswick players could stay at his new pub, or with friends, overnight, so travelling arrangements were made accordingly.

I believe eight of the team were Norman Wilson, John Moore, Charles Lowe, Tony Salisbury, Eric Whitehead, Geoff Davis, Evan Parry-Jones and Des Broomfield. Two are unknown, but there was also a young 'star', Miller, who'd just left Brighton College having scored stacks of runs, and was playing his first game in club cricket.

To save petrol, they travelled in four cars, one of which intended to return on the day, and everything went to plan on the outward journey. With a noon start, a salad lunch was laid on for all players and guests, which included the Chief Constable of Reading, a friend of the Davis family. I could trace no details of the cricket, and it appears the player's memories of this, were wiped out by the post match activities.

Everyone, including friends and spectators, went along to the 'Jack of Both Sides' after the match, and the jug was circulated rapidly, in an evening of uninhibited drinking. During this revelry, two off-duty nurses were enticed into the fray, though eyes swivelled upwards and mouths shut, when I tried to prise more details of this aspect from the players involved.

As closing time approached, the question arose as to where they could continue their socialising. With his local knowledge, Geoff Davis suggested a drinking club on an island in the Thames, and described the necessary route. The first car away contained Norman Wilson, Charles Lowe, Tony Salisbury and Eric Whitehead plus a Reading player and one nurse. They seemed to have found the place first time when they reached the river bank, as they saw a lighted building on an island.

The only available 'transport' to get across the water were two large rowing boats, moored on the nearby bank, and it was decided to 'commandeer' one of these for the trip. Amid much hilarity, the six negotiated the crossing in near darkness, the lighted building their only beacon. Having moored up, and flushed with the success of their rowing teamwork, they strode confidently through the entrance lobby of the building. Noisily sorting out their first round, they were well into the main hall before they twigged something was amiss; there was an Old Age Pensioner's bridge match in progress. The Steward was not amused, and ordered them out instantly, coupled with a threat to call the police.

Giggling uncontrollably they made their way back, and clambered into the boat, except Salisbury, held up for a call of nature. When he got there the others were already on their way, so to demonstrate his athleticism, he tried to jump the eight foot gap between bank and stern. Obviously a landlubber, when he landed the boat rocked violently, and shipped a huge volume of water. Indeed, after it settled down, and Salisbury had been screechingly abused, it was noted the water levels inside and outside the craft were much the same.

Exerting his authority as Brunswick skipper, Norman Wilson urged his crew to grit their teeth and pull together for the other bank, some forty yards away, Also, he nobly stated that as captain he would do his duty and was prepared if necessary, to go down with his ship.

As things got a bit fraught, the odd swear word was added to the shouting, shrieks and hilarity, waking nearby cottage residents, one of whom phoned the police. At this moment P.J. (Evan Parry-Jones) arrived in the second car, and remembers being greeted with a disjointed and fading chorus of 'Abide with me', floating up from the river.

Though no formal order to abandon ship was issued, the boat finally sank a few yards from the bank. In the ensuing mayhem, most of the crew sobered up enough to swim ashore, but Charles Lowe was laughing so much, he was in serious risk of drowning. Sadly, it appears all chivalry was cast aside when the nurse slipped into the water, not to be seen or heard of again.

At this point the police arrived, to join the scrum of scrambling survivors, thirsty cricketers and irate residents. With Tony Salisbury the first to be questioned, the others thought it great fun to also volunteer the name 'Salisbury' when their turn came, – it's not on record whether the police appreciated this humour. Precisely what happened next is unclear, but the following fallout is established.

Charles Lowe, having finished a heated altercation with a resident, went back to town with P.J. and Salisbury and booked into a hotel for the night. They used the room to change from their wet clothing into cricket gear, then noticed the corridor outside the room was about thirty yards long. Then two o'clock in the morning, Lowe padded up and proceeded to knock on the doors of the sleeping guests, loudly urging them to get up, and come and try to bowl him out.

When the third car arrived at the river, the police had got matters under control, and were in no mood for more games. The occupants were processed and dispersed briskly, but somehow the debutant Miller found himself arrested, and invited to cool down for the night in a cell at Reading Police Station. After this traumatic episode, it's a fact the young Miller never went anywhere near the Brunswick again, and it's possible his first game in club cricket was also his last.

Norman Wilson managed to escape the police at the river and drove off to return to Brighton alone. He stopped at a layby to change his clothes, for some reason putting on pyjamas rather than the available cricket gear in the boot. As he drove into Horsham around one o'clock, he noticed he was running out of petrol and took his second illogical step. Unable to find a filling station open, he pulled up alongside the only person he could see about; a policeman on foot patrol!

Having explained there were no filling stations open at that time of night, the constable developed an interest in Norman's pyjamas, and shone his torch around and into the car, noting the wet clothes spread out on the back seat. The following legendary dialogue was then supposed to have taken place:

'Excuse me sir, why are those clothes wet?'

'Well actually officer, I've just fallen into a river.'

'Oh I see. And why are you wearing pyjamas sir?'

'I thought I'd be well prepared officer, just in case I fell asleep at the wheel.'

In fact the constable didn't ask about the pyjamas and seemed satisfied enough to allow him to carry on from his first answer. Norman got home without running out of fuel, but the next day there were repercussions to be sorted out.

An anxious Geoff Davis rang him in the morning, to tell him the Chief Constable had been on the phone to state: the police had received a number of complaints, the owner of the sunken boat was going to sue, and there were likely to be prosecutions for 'disturbing the peace', at the very least. What's more, the registration number of Norman's car had been circulated to all forces and a cordon thrown around three counties.

After a succession of heated calls, things eventually calmed down and the police convinced it was all a bit of harmless fun, with no criminal intent. The boat was raised and refloated, with the owner placated by an offer of £5 towards the cost of a new oar, as the old one had drifted off downstream.

A surprising post-script to this story was that the fixture was not cancelled, and the next year the Chief Constable was called upon to say a few words of welcome to the Brunswick after lunch. His speech included the sentence, more of an instruction than an invitation: 'We all look forward to a most enjoyable game, but I trust the Brunswick will arrange their after match celebrations outside the Reading police area.'

CHAPTER 5

NOEL BENNETT

Noel Bennett was one of the great characters of club cricket in the Brighton and Hove area, and at one stage of his long career his fame spread to a wider audience. Born in 1909 and brought up in a cricketing family, he was always proud of the fact he was a direct descendant of John Small, the stone-walling batsman of Hambledonian times.

His father skippered and organised the Brighton Electricity XI, based in Preston Park, and when Noel left school in '26 he joined in the action. Initially he tried fast bowling, but the physical effort, coupled to a lifelong respiratory complaint, soon made him give up, and he settled down to become a slow right-arm spinner. Steadily, over the years, he slowed down further, so that after World War Two he became a lob bowler. With the recent trend to League cricket, I suspect lob bowling's a dying art, and Noel's story is of interest, for that reason alone.

Cricket was Noel's lifelong passion; he probably played nearly 2000 matches in his 45 seasons, and liked to point out he'd taken around 1500 wickets, no mean achievement for a bowler of his type. He played regularly into his sixties and when finally forced to give up, maintained his involvement with the game, by assisting the Sussex Scorer at the County Ground

When he started playing, and between the Wars generally, the centre for club cricket in Brighton was Preston Park, and this became Noel's home ground throughout his career. Learning the basics under his father's captaincy, he took over as Brighton Electricity skipper, and organiser of Noel Bennett's XI, during the War. His wider fame was achieved, as a result of events after the '39 season, which had passed by peacefully, with the full complement of matches.

With war being waged, by the time April '40 came round most local club cricketers had been called up, or were unable to play. By sheer enthusiasm, Noel and a few cronies, got together sides to play matches in Preston Park, mainly between Brighton Electricity and

St. Mary's, another old established Club.

Six games were played over the season, the results standing at three all after the last fixture in early October. To find a winner, it was agreed to arrange a match on Boxing Day, subsequently switched to Christmas Day to coincide with Noel's birthday.

At that time, it was probably the only match to be played on Christmas Day anywhere in the country, though there were a number of regular fixtures on Boxing Day.

The teams were called Noel Bennett's XI and the Yule Logs, with the game starting at ten o'clock sharp, and restricted to twenty overs per side. There were no limits on runs per batsmen or overs per bowler, and Noel always insisted that the match be played as 'a proper game of cricket'.

Not only was the first match a great success, but it became established as a regular fixture, and something of a social outing for players and spectators, to build an appetite for Christmas dinner.

Presumably life was dull for a sports reporter during the War, and one suspects, scouring for any material, the young Eamonn Andrews came across this event and started the publicity ball rolling. In the second or third year, the B.B.C. reported the match and basic details were also broadcast on the World Service.

Indeed, a friend of Noel's in Hong Kong on business, was staggered to listen to a match report on Boxing Day, featuring his pal playing in Preston Park. From then on the match became an annual media event, useful for providing light hearted material for the Christmas period, with television moving onto the scene later on.

In the first fifty years, Noel played in all but two matches when he was forced to stand down through illness, with just seven games rained off, or deemed unplayable.

My old schoolmaster Noel Jones recorded the best bowling performance, taking 9 for 23 in '47, and it's not difficult to imagine his spin and pace being devastating on a soggy, uneven pitch. His spell included the remarkable feat of taking five wickets with the first five balls of an over, (three bowled, two caught), something rarely achieved in any type of cricket.

I was fortunate to see the batting record being established in '78,

Noel Bennett demonstrates his trusty forward push, on his 80th birthday
Brighton Gazette

when Ron Faith scored a masterly 76 on a muddy pitch. Blocking anything straight, he scored rapidly with the sound technique of keeping the ball in the air.

There were many outstanding performances over the years, and apart from the conditions, it should be remembered the teams were out of practice, not having played for three months. It says much for his bowling skills that when Peter Beecheno arrived one year, heavily hung over from a Christmas Eve session, he still managed a first over maiden, all six deliveries on perfect line and length.

I played in the match for seven years from '65 and gained valuable experience of playing cricket in adverse, if not to say farcical, conditions. Apart from the odd mild dry year, when the pitch was no worse than a typical summer's day, the playing surfaces could be divided roughly into three categories.

First and most common would be for the pitch to be soft and saturated, the surface churning into liquid mud as the match progressed. For batsmen, this meant it became impossible to move the feet, and most deliveries would skid through at ankle height.

As it happened, these conditions perfectly suited my normal batting style, which I could summarise as too much right hand, and insufficient backlift. I was well equipped therefore, to chop or hack the ball away, as it skidded through, without getting bowled in mid-stroke. Indeed one year, I scored 20 out of 40 all out, a feat of which I remain proud to this day, especially as we'd played 12 a side.

For bowlers, footholds were the main problem, though this could be overcome by shortening the run-up, taken at a walking pace. Sawdust was normally available, and with liberal use a kind of paste mat would be formed around the crease.

A muddy game I recall, perhaps the most liquid of my involvement, resulted in no fewer than seven run-outs in one innings. It was not so much the batsmen being unable to turn, as that was a reckless move anyway, but more a question of being unable to set off.

The second pitch type was when the ground was frozen hard which, depending on the amount and timing of its preparation, could produce a lightning fast, flat track, worthy of a Test match strip. More likely however, was the pitch being unprepared before freezing, which meant all heelmarks and wormcasts became set like concrete, posing frightening problems to the batsmen.

There are two much re-told anecdotes about this situation. One year, the umpires went out to put the stumps in and unable to make any impression in the ground, had to return to find a mallett. Armed with a suitable implement, they were still forced to hammer away for several minutes, the sound echoing round the Park.

Then there was the occasion Peter Beecheno was heard chortling with glee, at the sight of frozen wormcasts on a length. 'Put 'em in Noel, put 'em in', he urged as Noel went to toss up. When this came about, batting against Beecheno that day was like facing a slip cradle sunk into a length, with the added hazard of getting the odd straight ball.

The other type of pitch was the snow covered, and though there's rarely snow on Christmas Day, there may be a fair amount lying around from the preceeding week. That was certainly the case at least once in my time, also devilishly cold with a biting wind.

Priority for all players was to wrap up with every available piece of clothing, and hip flasks were a useful accessory. I devised my own insulating system by putting on pyjamas, ends sealed into socks and gloves, before layers of shirts, trousers and sweaters were added.

At this point, I could make a lame joke about having played 'pyjama cricket', years before modern professionals ever knew the meaning of the term.

For a snow match, the pitch was swept in the morning, often leaving a surprisingly good playing surface with difficulties much as already described. But the additional snag for batsmen, was that the most powerful ground stroke, textbook or otherwise, could end up as a snowball on the edge of the square. Essential technique therefore, was to try and keep the ball in the air, easier said than done if it skidded through low.

In one of the Christmas Day matches, I made my unheralded debut as a television performer. One of the T.V. companies used to send down a crew from London to get a few shots, as a minor news item for Boxing Day. Though they were probably on triple time, the crew made it pretty clear they were bored with the whole exercise, knowing their trip was just for a few seconds of film.

They took some pictures of Noel, on his way to the wicket to toss up, and then hung around impatiently for the game to start. Noel's XI batted first and, as I'd been selected to open, I found myself facing the first ball of the match.

The crew probably wanted the stumps spreadeagled, or a spectacular boundary struck, though I preferred the latter prospect. Fortunately it turned out to be a juicy full toss on leg stump, which I managed to steer, rustily, down to deep square leg for two.

This was good enough for the cameramen, who packed up immediately, and within two minutes were seen leaving the ground. Thus anyone awake and not blinking excessively, could have seen my screen debut on the local early Boxing Day news.

When I first met Noel in the early '60's, he'd become a roly-poly figure with a distinctive waddling gait. Totally unathletic, he made matters worse by peering down his nose through glasses, giving the impression he had difficulty in seeing anything. 'King of the Park' and known to every cricketer in the Brighton area, he also featured regularly in the local press.

Nearing the end of his forty-five year playing span, he'd become a very slow lob bowler, of considerable guile. Apart from his near vertical trajectory, his distinctive bowling action was such he could fit the whole of his run-up, delivery stride and follow-through, between the creases, with something to spare.

The combination of age, appearance, run-up and field placing, not only lured unwitting batsmen into a state of jovial over-confidence, but could also induce feelings of sympathy in the softer hearted. Behind the facade, Noel had great confidence in his lob bowling skill, and it enabled him to ensnare many a headstrong young batsman with embarrassing ease.

Noel's bowling, which could lead to figures of 2 for 35 off three overs, was always likely to be expensive. Though automatically skipper of Bennett's XI, he liked to appear modestly reluctant to put himself on to bowl. In hard fought matches, his team mates would hold a mid-field conference, to decide whether they'd allow him to do just that. This event was useful in itself, as it could sow all manner of suspicion and doubts in the minds of the batsmen.

On the field, Noel would position himself at mid-off or mid-on, using his boots to good effect. He would always bat down the order, usually eleven, and his range of strokes began and ended with a forward defensive push. From the boundary, this shot could look textbook, till it became clear that he'd played down the wrong line, well after the ball had passed.

By the the mid-'60's Noel Bennett's XI had become a very useful side, its Sunday fixtures including some of the best village and town clubs in the County. In this golden period, I well remember the first match against St. James's in Stanmer Park.

We batted first on a pleasant day and, well aware of Noel's reputation, were determined to play each ball on its merits, when he came on to bowl. After making a solid start, our tactics were to accelerate and post a big total by tea. Everything went to plan, until Noel was allowed to give himself a whirl from the bottom end.

There was much arm waving and fussing about, as he meticulously positioned seven men round the boundary, all helping to increase the impatience of the waiting batsmen. Finally under way, the game's tempo went up a gear, with much scampering between wickets, and hits and mis-hits to the outfield. Though runs came rapidly, it was not without cost, and when I went out to bat Noel had already picked up three wickets.

I was determined not to do anything stupid, concentrating on picking up ones and twos to keep the scoreboard rolling. The first ball was well pitched up, and waiting patiently for it to come down, pushed it back carefully with straight bat. Likewise the second and third deliveries, but with growing sense of impatience; surely this was being ridiculously cautious? There was after all, no need to hand Noel the initiative and make him look unplayable.

As the fourth ball was launched, the blood rushed to my head, and I found myself racing down the pitch out of control. Some five yards down, I stopped and took an almighty heave, with no real idea of where the ball was, or where it was likely to land. Swinging the bat right over my shoulders, it hit the ground behind me as the ball landed alongside, and bounced gently towards the stumps.

For a split second, I toyed with the idea of trying to out-sprint the ball to the wicket, and deflect it away from the stumps. Playing a hockey shot, I could have done this, if I got a firm grip into my first stride.

But I gave up the idea, apart from the indignity of it all, there was the real possibility of demolishing the stumps and flattening the wicketkeeper in the process. I accepted my fate and trudged off to the boundary, completely humiliated, concentrating my thoughts on dreaming up a plausible excuse, for when the derision started.

From memory, Noel took about 5 for 45 by tea, which restricted our total and set up a win for his side. My dismissal highlighted one of the subtle aspects of lob bowling; playing defensive shots embarrassed the batsman, making it a virility test to try and smash each ball out of the park.

In fact, to play a ball dropping slowly and near vertically, at different points down the pitch, needed concentration, patience and footwork. An experienced, disciplined player would get to the pitch, and drive the ball straight to long-on or long-off, for an easy single. I remember the great Gerry Jarman doing just that to every ball he received in three overs, while his team mates urged him to, 'Get on with it', from the boundary.

On and off the field, Noel took a great deal of ribbing from his team mates, suffering taunts and indignities with good humour. As captain, he took the tactical aspects of a game very seriously, and, in moments of crisis, could be seen pacing round the boundary with furrowed brow, all of which led to further baiting from his colleagues.

A prime example of this ragging took place one day, when Noel was well into a bowling stint, with the game finely poised. He tossed up another high altitude lob, inducing the batsman to race too far down the pitch, from where he could only hammer the ball back up into the heavens.

With the ball soaring upwards, Noel shouted a highly optimistic, 'Mine!', a call greeted with unrestrained derision from the other fielders. As he shuffled about, peering myopically upwards, he tripped himself up, knocking off his glasses in the process.

Scrambling around on all fours trying to find them, some of the more sympathetic fielders started to move in, to take over the catching chance. But they'd only closed in a few yards, when they were stopped dead in their tracks, by a stern command from the square leg, 'Leave it! 'e called for it; let's see if it hits 'im!'.

As Noel cowered on the ground, covering back of head with hands, the ball plummetted to earth two feet away, to his relief, and the other's mock annoyance.

Noel's memories of amusing incidents, go back to the days when transport to matches was mostly undertaken by bus. A bit before my time, he tells two stories, the first of which resulted in his XI, losing their regular fixture against Findon.

For this away fixture, Bennett's XI met, as arranged, at Brighton Bus Station, to find their service cancelled as the crew hadn't turned up. As their sole means of private transport was one elderly, 125cc, BSA Bantam motorbike, it was decided Peter Beecheno and Gordon Holman would be despatched, as an advance party, to warn Findon of the XI's late arrival.

The massively overloaded bike, eventually chugged into the ground about the two thirty start time, and the Findon skipper was appraised of the situation. Though initially placated, the Findon skipper was beginning to lose his patience by three thirty, when he spied a 'crocodile' of players, struggling with kit and club bag, up the hill to the east of the ground.

Having marched heavily laden, from the bus stop on the main Worthing to London road, the players were in no condition to start rushing about in the field, and made that crystal clear to their skipper. Noel went out to toss up, making profuse apologies to the Findon skipper on the way and, no doubt, mentioning how much they'd looked forward to the fixture.

Obviously, the astute decision would have been to put the opposition in, had he won the toss, but Noel was mindful of the reception he might receive in his own changing room. The tension between the two sides therefore, was not improved when Noel won the toss and batted.

The wicket was not easy, well exploited by the Findon bowlers, and in the seventy-five minutes before tea, Bennett's XI struggled to 80 for 8, which Noel judged insufficient for a declaration. It need hardly be stated that inter club relations were not improved when Noel revealed his intention, the news received with incredulity by the opposition.

In a violent thrash after tea, another 50 were added, to leave Findon an hour and a quarter to score 130 odd. Psychologically of course, this was the perfect situation for Noel's lobs, as the Findon batsmen, generally fed up, were champing at the bit to get on with it.

Putting himself on after a few opening overs, Noel astutely placed six men on the boundary between deep square leg and long-on. Almost from his first ball, he created mayhem as batsman after batsman, each in some degree of anger, committed suicide in the run chase. He grabbed eight wickets as his XI wrapped up the match, with overs and runs to spare. The team enjoyed a convivial session in the local pub afterwards, without sight of their opposition!

His second anecdote highlighted a major problem, when making a long bus journey to away matches. They were playing at Warnham, near Horsham, one year, and got involved in a marathon session after the game, having to drink up and dash out to catch the last bus home.

By the time they neared Henfield, which had involved a change of buses at Horsham, several of the players were bursting for a pee, and the driver was persuaded to stop and wait for them. The bus-stop was by the Henfield cricket ground and, for the sake of decorum, the six in need of relief jumped off and scrambled through the rough grass, to get away from the well-lit bus.

In high spirits and pitch darkness, when they got to the outfield, someone suggested they might as well go all the way to the square; the track was always a batsman's paradise, so a little added moisture might assist the spinners! This idea found immediate favour, with much banter about improving the track, and 'pissing all over them'.

Of course, no-one from Henfield was around, as they'd long since locked up and gone home. So, a terrible act of desecration took place, amid shrieks of pleasure and relief, on one of the most venerable grounds in the County. (It is a fact; the following day Henfield declared with 212 for 2 at tea!)

By coincidence, one of the few games I guested for Noel, turned out to be a delightful muddle of a match, and I still recall the basic details. Without knowing the actual scores, I believe my estimates are accurate enough, to give a full picture of a game played in the best traditions of 'friendly' club cricket.

It was on the Thursday of Southwick's cricket week in August '68, an all day match on the Green. Heavy rain the previous day had wiped out that match, and left the wicket barely playable for our game. The pitch surface, dark brown soft mud, had been rolled flat, and though drying rapidly was clearly going to cause problems in the early stages.

With a prompt eleven thirty start, Southwick batted first and immediately struggled with the combination of pitch and the new ball, swinging and wobbling about in the humid atmosphere. Wickets fell regularly, and by the one o'clock lunch interval, the home side had slumped to 93 for7. Twenty minutes after lunch, the tail was cleaned up and Southwick all out for 110.

Bennett's XI opened their innings with two experienced and free scoring batsmen, Peter Streeter and Peter McArthur. Streeter, a hard hitting driver, and McArthur, a fleet-footed accumulator, made batting look easy from the start, putting on ninety for the first wicket in just over an hour. Fifteen minutes later it was all over, and we'd won by 8 wickets by quarter to four.

Pointedly, the umpires left the stumps in as the players trooped off, and Noel sauntered out to meet the Southwick skipper, to dicuss a possible beer match. After head scratching and bit of friendly chat, both men returned to their teams, to sow the seeds of the muddle.

Essentially, the Southwick skipper believed the match had become a two innings affair, and there was therefore, everything to play for. Noel told us we'd won the proper match, but were going to bat on to give everybody a knock, and we'd play it by ear from then on.

It seemed a vague, pointless exercise, but we had to do something, being nearly three hours before opening time. In the forty minutes before the four thirty tea interval, we mucked about swinging the bat to get ourselves out, and declared eight down, with a first innings lead of 70.

When Southwick started their second innings with two and a half hours left, Noel began to have serious doubts about what rules he'd agreed. Noticing they'd kept the same batting order, he responded by putting on our opening bowlers, and told us he wanted proper fielding.

From then on, the match became a close fought contest, as we tried hard to restrict their total. But we still had slightly the upper hand, and after 80 minutes play got them all out again for 120.

This left us the simple task of scoring 50 in an hour, and we relaxed; there being much banter about how Noel should select the batting order. The consensus was, all names be drawn from a hat, but Noel, with customary caution, insisted we kept our normal openers.

Streeter and McArthur were a little embarrassed by this situation, and adopted a cavalier approach from the start. Such was their mastery on the day however, they put on 42 in no time at all, when Streeter gave his wicket away. Things slowed a little as the second wicket pair added a few runs, and at 48 McArthur was bowled trying to finish off the game.

Our batsman drawn four was normally a tailender, so the Southwick skipper, with true tenacity and dogged optimism, brought back his best bowlers in a last gasp attempt to save the day. A confident single from the next ball however, took the score to 49 for 2, with just one needed. Laughter then greeted a tremendous cross-batted heave, as our number four made his first ball exit, signalling my entry on the scene.

Before I went out, Noel and others had a quiet word with me, saying everyone had had a good laugh, but now was the time to wrap things up sensibly, so we could start some serious drinking. I strode to the wicket, determined to demonstrate my cool head and great experience in these situations, by simply waiting for the right ball.

By then overcast and cool, as I reached the crease, an attacking field had been set, and the Southwick bowlers were giving it all they'd got. I pushed forward carefully to the first two, and though accurate, the bowling seemed pretty straight up and down. When the third ball arrived my brain snapped, up went my head, I made a horrendous ya-hoo, and was comprehensively bowled.

Shamed, I trudged back to the boundary, head bowed, simply unable to dream up a viable excuse. But worse was to come; my example was followed in more or less the same fashion, by the next five batsmen. In a sequence of collective suicide the like of which I've never seen before or since, we contrived to slump from 49 for 2, to 49 for 9, chasing 50 to win!

As this hari-kari had been going on, Noel had been pacing the boundary, unable to believe what he was seeing. He'd learned to live with his normal worries at each match, but this situation was ridiculous. In a state of shock, he allowed himself to be strapped into pads and kitted out, to try and stave off an ignominious moral defeat.

As I watched him waddle out to bat, over-sized pads flapping at the knees, cap clamped down over glasses, in the gathering gloom; I can't think of another occasion when the appearance and demeanour of a new batsman inspired less confidence. Completing a zig-zag approach, he took time over his guard, while all fielders were summoned up and positioned within a few yards.

With spots of rain adding to Noel's problems, the bowler, having pointedly lengthened his run-up, rushed in for the first delivery. With tension unbearable, most of us were unable to watch as, predictably, Noel played his forward push. The ball hit his front pad above the knee, and richoteted down to fine leg, as the fielders erupted in a crescendo of screamed appeals.

With respect to club umpires, I assume it must have been our man at the bowlers wicket, as it was not given, and Noel struggled down the pitch for a single. The relief on the faces of the errant batsmen like myself was visible, and Noel was welcomed back like a conquering hero.

It was a superb climax to a lovely game, and celebrations soon commenced in the 'Cricketer' pub by the Green. Tactfully, as we'd won under either playing rules, there were no discussions about this aspect with the Southwick players. But I think if Noel had been out first ball, I'd have given the pub a miss!

I went to see Noel, to glean some stories, when he was into his eighties and living in a boarding house in Hove. Arriving in my normal casual (scruffy) clothes, I was embarrassed to find him waiting for me, smartly dressed in grey three piece suit, as if meeting someone important.

With three bulky scrapbooks under one arm, he was fully prepared for any question, as we meandered through his long cricket career. Time permitting, I could have stayed for hours, and ended punch drunk with bowling statistics!

Noel Bennett died in June 1994 and I attended his funeral in Brighton a week later, on a glorious, hot, sunny day.

There were over 50 people present and, as he'd never married and had no family, almost every one was a local club cricketer. After the ceremony, which included a moving eulogy from Derek Linford, old acquaintances were renewed and the reminiscences flowed.

There was no sadness; it was almost a celebration that we'd all played a part in, and been touched by, the life of such a lovely man.

I'd only been involved in about twenty games of cricket with Noel, and therefore knew relatively little about him. Yet to me, Noel was the embodiment of uninhibited enthusiasm for the game, and this occasion was more than the putting to rest of a great character on the local scene. In a personal way, it seemed also to draw a line under the fun days of 'friendly' club cricket.

CHAPTER 6

THREE SUPERSTARS

Though I've usually mentioned the 'stars' in a facetious sense, there are three players who, in different ways, I regard as giants of Sussex club cricket in my time. About ten years older than me, had the circumstances been right they could certainly have played first class cricket, and probably starred in that as well.

There's an element of hero worship in this, and certainly I'd have swapped my career with any of their's. But they were also considerable personalities, generating some fine humorous moments, and for these reasons I put them in the true 'superstar' category.

TREVOR ADCOCK played most of his cricket for Steyning and Henfield, and is one of that select band who've scored a hundred centuries in their career. A tall, strongly built man, he was a naturally gifted all-rounder, in some ways perhaps, a local club cricket Sobers. Scoring freely as a left-handed batsman, he bowled swift right arm in his early days, switching to leg spin after a knee injury.

With normal time for a side's innings about two and a half hours, to score a century in club cricket it's obviously easier to open the batting, and you can't play yourself in for too long. It also helps if you're on a small ground, with hard, true wicket, and of course, against weak opposition.

Trevor never opened the batting, scoring most of his 102 centuries from number three. Though he often got to the crease quickly, a wicket would have fallen, so initial caution was necessary. For the rest, he went in down the order to as low as six.

Again, to do the double in club cricket is not too difficult for the batting part, but much more so on the bowling front. It means about two wickets a game, but of course the opposition wouldn't lose all their wickets each innings. Trevor did the double in 15 seasons, surely a tremendous feat that puts his all-round abilities in perspective.

When I asked him about the highlights of his career, as expected he was suitably modest and forgetful. But I did prise out details of a match in 1960, of which clearly, he remains proud.

It was for Steyning against Findon, with the home side batting first. The teams were evenly matched, Trevor soon going in at three, but the other batsmen struggling to make headway. However, that didn't matter much, because when Steyning declared at tea with 197 for 6 on the board, Trevor was 171 not out!

When he'd finished the tale he threw in a postscript:

'Of course, I soon came down to earth; in my next game I was stumped third ball for a duck!...', adding the casual afterthought, '...though I did get all ten wickets.'

St. James's played Steyning regularly in the '60's and were often put to the sword by Trevor. A strong memory from those days, was the occasion I was fielding at deep long on near the tennis courts on their ground. Steyning had a substantial playing area with the outfield sloping down from the table, and I was the best part of a hundred yards from the bat.

With his side needing quick runs after tea, Trevor wasted no time tackling the task when he got to the wicket. Always with plenty of time to play his shots, effortless backswing, and tremendous power, he was soon crashing the ball low over the infield, in the arc between mid on and extra cover.

Launching into another drive, I could see it coming my way, and realised it was a horrendous catching chance. Then at the peak of my physical strength and fitness, I decided to run forward a few yards, jump up, and push my stronger right hand forward above my head, pressing the left behind.

It nearly came off, but my hands were an inch too far to the right, and the ball ripped them apart and burst through. I remember feeling shock and disappointment, twisting round quickly to see it bounce once before racing over the boundary and on down the hill.

Trevor Adcock was respected throughout the County for his skills and talent. He was also a quiet, self effacing sportsman, who always unselfishly put his team first. My ideal superstar.

PETER BEECHENO was undoubtedly the greatest bowler I played with, a fine middle order batsman, and a character known far and wide in the south of England. Also, as a true cricket fanatic, his career perfectly illustrates the all consuming enthusiasm for the game during the post war boom.

In order to get some facts on his remarkable playing career, we met to reminisce in '94, and I was amazed at the detail he could recall of matches stretching back to the Second World War.

As an uncoached 14 year old, his first game was filling in for Noel Bennett's XI in Preston Park in '44, after which he played regularly for that team and Brighton Electricity. Rapidly learning the essential skills, in the '50's he also started playing midweek for the Brunswick and Brighton Council XI. Playing Saturday and Sunday, and with evening games as well, he was regularly notching up over 60 matches a season.

To raise his standard, he joined Brighton and Hove in '55, and played in probably the strongest club side in Sussex of that generation. Stacked with stars it was often said that number five rarely batted, with the bowling strength just as formidable.

Looking for more action, Beech switched to St. James's in the early '60's, playing every fixture and becoming Club captain, before he left the area in '69. Joining Streatham in the Surrey League, he became a leading player, till in '73 he moved abroad for health reasons. Switching to Holland in '78, he then landed the job of Coach to the

Dutch National Women's Team, a position he held for 10 years.

The raw statistics of his 50 year cricket career are to me, quite staggering. Though clearly not accurate figures, it's a considered estimate that he's played over 2000 matches, scored 35000 runs and taken 4000 wickets.

When I first played with him, he was at the height of his powers, and had developed a repertoire of comments, mannerisms and ploys, to 'psych' out batsmen. Watching these being used was most enjoyable, and I sketch these below with some memorable anecdotes.

Beech batted left handed, and was particularly strong on the back foot, playing very straight with bat close to body. He would surely have scored a lot more runs, but was usually put in down the order, as he was in such demand in his bowling role.

When brought on to bowl, he would stride briskly to the wicket, ripping off a sweater on the way, with body language that said, 'Right, now let's get down to business.' Right arm medium pace, he bowled off a ten yard run-up, with a plodding flat-footed approach. His action was very square-on, with a slightly round arm delivery, but it was at the end of his short follow through that the real theatrics started.

If the batsman was beaten for pace, he would end poised on one leg, hand near the ground, in classic pose. If it shaved the stumps he would throw up his arms in dismay, and remain in a state of utter incredulity for some seconds, while emitting a string of 'phews', 'cors' and 'ahs'. And for the unsuccessful forward grope, he would exhibit amazement, then call out the mocking, light-hearted 'Well left!'

Underneath all this Beech had, over the years, developed superb control of line and length. At the beginning of a spell, he would experiment with off and leg cutters, in and out swing, and seamers, all of which he could bowl to order. After a few overs, he would make up his mind which was best for the day, reset his field, and carry on from there.

If he reckoned to be on a shirt front, with no help from the elements, he would bowl seam up, while slowing to use variations in pace and flight. This he could do without perceptible change in action.

One of his favourite ploys in this mode, when a batsman was in attacking mood, was simple and often successful. He would bowl the first three balls of an over just short of a drivable length on off stump, with mid-off and mid-on in orthodox positions. Then he would discreetly signal the two fieldsmen to go deeper, as he walked back for the next deliveries. For the last ball he would give a meaningful nod, implying this was the one they could expect a catch.

I remember two occasions this trick worked when I was at mid-off. Sure enough, the first time the batsman spooned a gentle catch to me, and with heart pounding and huge relief, I safely held it.

The other was chipped to mid-on, and the fielder, trying too hard to do everything right, spilled the chance. Mortified, he sank to his knees, head in hands, while Beech indicated total disbelief. It says much for his sportsmanship, that he made no audible comment on this outcome, though what he was saying to himself must have been unprintable.

It was the end of a long weary week for Beech, when he arrived at Stanmer for the St. James's Saturday match against Rottingdean. A couple of mid-week games with heavy evening sessions, had left him in need of an easy ride for this derby match. But a quick glance round the changing room confirmed his fears; we were short of bowling and he'd probably have to tie up one end for most of the innings.

It didn't help also, being a hot, sticky, windless day, making it hard for everyone to summon up the energy for physical effort. The match got underway with Rottingdean batting, and our first bowlers posed no serious threat in their opening spells.

When tired or in a bad mood, Beech would say little, leaving the banter and sparkle for others. So, when eventually called into action from the Church end, he trudged to the wicket and went through the motions with little enthusiasm. Wheeling away mechanically, his accuracy was enough to reduce the scoring rate, and he picked up the odd wicket as well.

With Rottingdean falling behind the clock and quick runs needed, a new batsman came to the wicket. A jaunty young chap, blond locks flowing from under multi-coloured cap, strode purposefully to the crease.

With the fielders visibly wilting, and reluctant to move anywhere, Beech took an inordinately long time setting his field. He went round each position, fussing over getting deep square to move a couple of yards to his left, and the precise depth of mid-on. He had particular trouble with long-off, who seemed to regard going deeper as a personal insult, but Beech would not budge till he was right back on the rope.

Satisfied at last, Beech started his next over to the new batsman, who played the first ball with an impeccable forward defensive. He repeated this for the second and third deliveries, dropping the ball dead in front of the bat.

Then to the fourth, he set his feet each side of the crease, and played what can only be described as a perfect, full-bloodied golf drive, with swinging backlift and follow through right over the shoulders. He timed and connected perfectly, sending the ball very high where it hovered, before drifting down to strike the Church tower a yard below the spire; as big a six as I've seen at Stanmer.

This provoked giggles and snide back-of-the-hand remarks among the fielders, supposedly out of earshot. Long-off however, couldn't resist the chance of embarrassing the bowler, and gleefully shouted the old chestnut: 'Quite sure you don't want me thirty yards further back, Beech?'

While all this was going on, and the ball being retrieved from the graveyard, Beech stood silent and expressionless by the crease. With chin up, he remained aloof to the taunts, which he wouldn't dignify with comment.

Ball returned, Beech scuttled in for his next delivery, to which the batsman fashioned an identical stroke, and was bowled middle stump. Of course, Beech had just held the ball back slightly, and that was that.

Whilst happy to get another wicket, it was galling to see Beech come out on top yet again. His reaction to this little victory was lovely. He said nothing, but turned slowly full circle, displaying an exagerrated, false grin.

It was an all day match at Godalming on a fine warm, July Sunday. The ground had a large, flat outfield which, with a well kept, high class table, usually gave little help to the bowling side.

St. James's were in the field and had picked up a couple of wickets before lunch, but the afternoon session was likely to be a long, hot ordeal. Beech had bowled half a dozen overs already, but was brought back immediately after the break, when the Godalming number four was getting into his stride. Clearly a 'star', he paid scant regard to Beech's reputation, setting about all the bowling with relish, and threatened to run riot unless checked.

Having raced into the forties, the 'star' suddenly quietened down, and the flow of scorching strokes dried up. Deadlock continued for twenty minutes or so before, desperate to score runs, he spooned a catch to mid on. Everyone rushed in to congratulate Beech, delighted at getting this key wicket, and relieved at the break from chasing leather.

Beech modestly lapped up the adulation then, at the appropriate moment, offered this classic hype as explanation:

'I thought I'd worked him out; I shifted it from middle and leg, to leg!'

Such was the respect with which he was held, everyone nodded sagely in agreement, while I struggled to choke back a guffaw of laughter. The difference between the two directions is just over two inches in 22 yards, and I doubt if the most accurate bowler of all time, could consistently pitch on one line or the other.

Beech was invited to play for the East Sussex County Council, in an all day Sunday match at the Blue Circle ground in Bromley. It was in part a business junket, with food and drink lavish and unlimited.

I'd played at Stanmer on the same day, which turned out baking hot, went to the County Oak pub afterwards, and was surprised to find Beech propping up the bar. He looked pale and exhausted and said nothing for some time. Finally I confronted him with a direct question as to whether he was alright. Painfully and slowly he managed a reply, which said it all:

'28 overs, 12 maidens, 1 for 42!'

St. James's played a fixture for three years against Middleton in the early '60's, all of which we won by a handsome margin. As they were a prestigious Club, later to become stalwarts of the Sussex League, this was something of a coup at the time. Beech revelled in the prospect of humbling the mighty, and I well remember one of the matches when he took a hatful of wickets.

It was a blustery day with a firm, drying pitch, and when we bowled first Beech was soon in his element, getting the ball to seam, swing and lift on demand. Though the Middleton batsmen struggled manfully, it was an uphill battle and wickets fell regularly.

A cocky young chap came out to bat, public school, fancy cap and all the rest, his body language indicating he was going to grit teeth, roll up sleeves, and generally sort things out. He took guard confidently, then faced up to Beech, 'pawing the ground' at the end of his run-up.

For the first ball he put down an outswinger, which lifted and was taken by the 'keeper chest high in front of first slip. To this the young chap played a determined forward push, but was some way from making contact.

Though before the era of sledging, Beech had a stock of derogoratory quips for most situations. For this he trotted out his jovial 'well left!', which somewhat irked our young chap, no doubt considering it 'bad form'.

Second ball was an off-cutter, which whipped back across the top of middle stump, taken by the 'keeper diving across to leg. Another textbook defensive grope got no nearer making contact, Beech commenting, 'well left again!'

Likewise the third ball, a leg cutter, to which the batsman stretched even further forward with bat heavily angled. Beech starting to chuckle, but only repeated, 'well left again!'

When the fourth ball resulted in another miss by a mile, it was becoming embarrassing. Never one to gloat, Beech let the funny side take over. Stopping at the end of his follow through, he stroked his chin and chuckled to himself before calling down the wicket:

'Tell you what old sport; you hold the bat still, and I'll try and hit it!'

We all thought it was a superb comment, perfectly timed, though our young chap remained distinctly unimpressed.

I like the story of a Sunday afternoon Benefit match on the County Ground Hove around 1950, when Brighton and Hove were invited to play a Sussex XI. In those days, big crowds would turn out for these fixtures, and a substantial collection made for the beneficiary.

From the boundary, it appeared to be a real contest, and every effort was made to maintain this illusion. Standard form was for the County to bat first, and score about 250, with some spectacular hitting at the end. The Visitors would then be allowed to get near the target, and an exciting finish engineered if possible.

In the changing room, Brighton and Hove were preparing to take the field, when the Sussex captain and beneficiary, James Langridge, popped in for a few words. He said in effect, the crowd wanted to see a proper game of cricket, so they could pull all the stops out to try and make it an entertaining contest.

Opening bowlers Beech and Peter Wales, needed no further encouragement, and knew all about the famous sea fret from the bottom end. Eagerly racing in, John Langridge was caught in the slips in the second over, and Don Smith, Ken Suttle and Alan Oakman were soon back in the pavilion.

James Langridge was at the wicket, when the Sussex score had slumped to 60 for 6, with serious prospect of a beer match having to be arranged. He strolled over to have a quiet word with the Brighton and Hove skipper: 'Enough is enough, the crowd has come to see Sussex bat, not Beecheno bowl. Take him off.'

Duly done, Sussex recovered to score about 160, then made sure the visitors were all out for less.

A lasting memory of Beech, the cricket fanatic and optimist, was from a late summer game at Storrington one year. It was a heavily overcast afternoon, and there'd been plenty of rain in the preceeding days to make the wicket soft and skiddy.

St. James's batted first and struggled manfully against accurate seam bowling. We declared at tea with 123 for 6, satisfied it would take outstanding batting by the home side to get the runs, especially with Beech in full flow.

Things worked much according to plan, Beech wheeling away from the top end, cutting the ball both ways, and generally in his element. We worked steadily through the Storrington order, and, all things being equal, expected to get them all out. Then from around six o'clock, the cloud cover got lower and darker, and with the light fading fast, the batsmen were having difficulty seeing the muddy ball, let alone hitting it.

Beech knew victory was within our grasp, but aware of the light and rain prospect, hurried impatiently back to his mark after each ball. An hour before close, with Storrington 66 for 6, the feared disaster happened; flashes of lightning and rumbling thunder were followed by torrential rain, and everyone rapidly took cover.

It might have been a sharp shower, but after twenty minutes or so, the rain if anything, was more intense, and play couldn't have resumed as by then the square was under water.

With the abandonment of the game taken as read, players on both sides changed and filtered through to the bar. I was about the last to do so, thankful for the solitary light bulb contrasting with the general gloom.

I went to the door for a final peep outside, and was surprised to find Beech, still in full kit, surveying the semi-darkness intensely. Querying what he was looking at, his measured reply, betraying disappointment with still lingering hope, was:

'You never know, the clouds are high!'

GERRY JARMAN, from my first sighting, looked the complete physical embodiment of the 'superstar' club cricketer. Around the time we were developing the 'domestic' concept, he'd recently returned from living in Africa and joined Montefiore C.C. I played against Gerry during the '70's, and with humour in mind, marked him out as someone to watch from our first game.

Immaculately turned out for every match, with freshly laundered shirt and flannels, and boots thoroughly whitened, he looked the part from head to toe, including an important looking, hooped blue cap. But his really distinguishing feature was his white, silk neckerchief, which he always wore knotted the same way, under turned up, shirt collar.

Gerry had a positive, clear voice, with slightly upper crust accent and an abundance of self confidence, based on some solid achievements in his prime. This was something which often irritated the opposition, but the fact had to be faced; he was a magnificent player, certainly capable of success in the first class game, had he so chosen.

He was a fair bowler, putting down a highly spun, looped leg break, from a theatrical, bouncy run-up. But primarily he was a batsman, with a complete range of strokes, which he played in unhurried, textbook fashion. Quick and light on his feet, he was equally at home going forward or back, and each shot was timed and stroked, never thumped.

John Bushell, his experienced skipper at Montefiore, paid him the considerable compliment by saying Gerry was the batsmen, from all Sussex club players, he would select to bat for his life.

From a brief acquaintance I've gleaned some delightful anecdotes, which really demonstrate he was a big fish in a small pond, when playing in local club cricket.

Gerry made his mark in the first game I played against him, at Stanmer, when we were batting first.

Having weighed up the bowling, in the third over Derek Pickering, our opening bat, took a couple of paces down the pitch and drove a ball sweetly along the ground, for four through the covers. It appeared to be a perfect shot and Derek, then at the height of his batting powers, was well satisfied with his efforts.

As everyone else admired the stroke, Gerry, fielding at second slip, strode up to Derek, shaking his head:

'No, no, no old boy; let me show you. It's like this!'

Derek stood there dumbfounded, as Gerry took his bat and proceeded to point out all the technical errors in his shot, coupled to much practical demonstration. Engrossed in his masterclass he was unaware the ball had been returned, so his skipper had to interrupt and order him back to the slips.

It was another afternoon match at Stanmer Park between St. James's and Hove Montefiore, and everyone was milling around in front of the House before the start. John Bushell the Montefiore captain, marshalled his men to go out and field, annoyed that Gerry hadn't turned up.

Suddenly a car appeared, raced up the approach drive, and skidded to a halt in the midst of the throng, with much crunching and spewing of gravel. As conversation halted, Gerry leapt out and stood momentarily surveying the scene. Halfway out to the middle, Bushell shouted angrily:

'I told you two thirty start Gerry; where've you been?'

'Goalf!!'

There was silence as the audience tried to fathom what this meant, then someone asked quietly;

'Where was that Gerry; East Brighton, West Hove, the Dyke?'

'No no no old boy; Persian Gulf. I've been out there taking tea with the Sheikh of Akhabar!'

In the same fixture another year, St. James's fielding first, two wickets fell quickly and Gerry was in before three o'clock. Playing himself in carefully, he started scoring easily, and in no time at all we were applauding his fifty.

During this period, there'd been a lovely incident when Gerry noticed that mid-off had fallen asleep. Standing flat-footed, arms crossed on chest and with vacant expression, the fielder was about level with the bowler's wicket when Gerry pushed a ball hard to him with the confident shout:

'Come one! He's well back on his heels!'

Stung into action, mid-off pounced on the ball and hurled it the bowler's stumps, well after Gerry had cruised home of course.

Gerry was never a spectacular batsman, or one to destroy an attack, so he continued effortlessly accumulating, playing each ball on its merits. With his full range of strokes, the score board ticked away merrily, and no one had any idea how many he'd got, as we approached tea. And to be fair, neither had he.

Montefiore had reached 200 and were certain to declare at the interval, when with one ball to go, Gerry facing, play was held up by a shout from the scorer:

'Gerry, you're on 95!'

Genuinely surprised, he walked towards the official and the following shouted dialogue ensued:

'How many did you say scorer?'

'95 Gerry.'

'Did you say 95?'

'Yes; 95 Gerry.'

'So that means I need a six for my hundred then?'

'That's right Gerry'

'And it's the last ball before tea?'

'Yes Gerry.'

'Right O.K. So it's six I want then.'

Listening to all this, we were getting extremely irritated, to put it mildly, and would have done anything to stop him getting the runs. The bowler was a medium paced youngster, and mid-off moved across for a quiet word of advice. Two others also ran up to offer their views, so by the time he started his run-up, he was thoroughly confused.

The result was of course, he over-pitched an attempted yorker, which Gerry had anticipated by walking down the wicket. With a dismissive, effortless sweep of bat across body, he despatched the full toss over the mid-wicket boundary, to thud into the stonework of Stanmer House at upper floor level. In the same movement he tucked bat under arm and continued striding towards the boundary.

Montefiore were batting one day, with Gerry padded up and waiting to go in at his usual number four. There was an element of aggro on the field, one or two things being said and done which Gerry considered 'not on'.

When his turn came go in, he strode out from the pavilion in belligerent mood, ready to teach lessons. As he reached the square, he announced to all and sundry:

'I hope you chaps are ready to chase leather this afternoon!'

I understand they did so.

Over the years I'd heard gossip about Gerry's cricketing deeds in Kenya and Hong Kong, with talk of centuries and 'seeing off' Fred Trueman. When I wrote up these stories I phoned him, to see if he could remember any details. A difficult conversation to start, as I hadn't had any contact with him for fifteen years, and he only vaguely knew who I was.

Pretending I was researching a weighty volume about great club cricketers, I got the discussion round to his hey-days in Africa:

'Was it true you scored a century against a side including Fred Trueman, for Kenya Kongonis?'

'Phew… thats going back a bit! I got several actually; the best one I thought was against 'd'Oliviera's lot'!'

'Against the Cavaliers?'

'Good grief, I can't remember now. It was the World XI I think.'

'So Trueman wasn't playing?'

'I played against Trueman certainly; a cracking one-dayer. They got 160 odd, and we were half a dozen short. Great game of cricket!'

During a lengthy chat, Gerry mentioned he'd got some press cuttings collecting dust in the attic. With my highly developed antenna for bullshit, I asked him, casually, if he would find the relevant ones and let me borrow them. When they arrived, I have to admit I was genuinely impressed.

'd'Oliviera's lot' were the International Cavaliers in a three day match against the East African Cricket Conference, at the Sikh Union Ground Nairobi in February '62. The Cavaliers batted first and got 346, to which E.A.C.C. replied with only 156.

Then Cavaliers scored 301 for 7 declared, leaving E.A.C.C. 492 to win. They nearly made it, being all out for 471 with Gerry, who opened the innings, being run out for 131.

To be fair, the local press reports referred to the Cavaliers as the 'World XI', and it was: Hanif Mohammed, E.Weekes, B.D'Oliviera, C.McDonald, T.Graveney, R.Marshall, S.Gupte, H.Stephenson, H.Larter, N.Gifford and Saeed Ahmed.

The 'cracking one-dayer' of which Gerry was particularly proud, was between the same sides at the same ground on 11th October '60. Cavaliers made 160, and Gerry scored 36 as the E.A.C.C. fought their way to 153 all out. A local report suggests it was a serious contest, which seems likely as Trueman took 7 for 36 and Statham 3 for 28.

Listed from the scorecard, the Cavaliers XI could be described as 'quite useful': R.Benaud, T.Graveney, G.Pullar, K.Barrington, N.O'Neill, R.Simpson, M.J.K.Smith, L.Maddocks, R.Illingworth, F.Trueman and B.Statham.

After success at that level, facing Noel Bennett in Preston Park couldn't have held too many terrors for Gerry. It went a long way to explain his supreme self-confidence at the crease, and the delicious arrogance of the lovely story given me by John Bushell.

Montefiore had arranged a new, all day Sunday fixture against Ockley, north of Horsham. It turned out to be one of those rare perfect, sweltering hot, summer days, complete with shimmering haze and the hum of insects.

Gerry arrived at the Ground and was instantly impressed with its attractive layout, stopping his car and striding off to inspect the track. A quick glance at that told him all he wanted to know, and, in expansive mood, he marched back towards the pavilion.

There were a number of senior Ockley club members sitting on benches outside, enjoying the sun as they waited the start. As he approached, Gerry announced cheerily:

'Good morning gentlemen; what a magnificent day for a game of cricket! I shall score a hundred today, and when I've done so, I'll buy you all a pint!'

Ockley won the toss and batted and things got under way in the usual fashion. A relevant point, it was noticed the home umpire was a stickler for the laws, stamping his authority on the match.

By mid-afternoon Ockley had reached 280 and declared, on what was clearly a perfect batting track. Montefiore set off on the run chase, with Gerry champing at the bit, due in at his usual number four. When he got to the wicket, the combative Ockley opening bowler was finishing his first spell, and immediately the two rubbed each other up the wrong way, with words being exchanged.

Getting into top gear, Gerry took full advantage of the conditions, cruising along to reach his century by the middle of the last session. But there were still more runs to be scored, and they'd left it a bit late, with a dozen needed from the last over. The opening bowler, brought back for a final fling, was also determined to do his damnest to stop them.

In a flurry of activity and rising tension, Gerry struck a six, the ball being lost in bushes. It took several minutes to find, and though at that point there was no doubt Montefiore needed four runs to win, the umpire was not entirely happy. With Gerry about to face the next ball he held up play and called to the boundary:

'Scorers; I'd like a check on the number of balls left please?' Tension rose further as they consulted their books and double-checked, before replying:

'Two balls left umpire!'

To this Gerry, glaring at the bowler, loftily and in ringing tones, threw down the gloriously provocative challenge:

'*One* will be quite sufficient!!'

Positively seething understandably, the bowler over-strained to deliver the unplayable ball he desperately wanted. Gerry was too quick for him, got down the wicket, and imperiously drove him between cover and extra for four, to wrap up the match.

CHAPTER 7

UMPIRES

When I first played club cricket, near the peak of the post-war boom, the sheer number of matches played under the old 'friendly' system, meant there were insufficient 'proper' umpires to go round. All sorts of odd bods got roped in to stand, whether or not they knew what they were doing, and well meaning retired players would turn out for their old club, to keep in touch, or watch their offspring in action.

If they'd played the game, they saw no need to polish up on the Laws, and if they hadn't, they were usually quite happy to play it by ear. There were of course some 'decent' Association umpires, proud of their knowledge and impartiality, and pretty serious about the whole thing, but at that time, in the minority.

Watching the antics of the umpires, was one of the joys of playing in that period, except when you were on the receiving end of an appalling L.B.W. Facetiously and unfairly, this led us to classify the men in white coats, as either bent or incompetent, or, worst of all, bent and incompetent.

There's a sackful of stories on this theme; the oldest chestnut in the first category being, 'how's that Dad?', 'well bowled son!'. I saw and heard that happen one day, but the family wisely omitted to use their names, so we only found out afterwards.

One of my favourites of the 'incompetent' category, concerned an earnest little spin bowler, when no-balled years ago. He had taken three short steps to the wicket, and stopped in his delivery stride with no follow through. His front foot was about six inches behind the batting crease, and back foot the same in front of the bowling line. The evidence was there to see, so he pointed to his front foot and said, with shocked indignation, 'What's wrong with that?'

Loftily the umpire replied, 'I'm not interested in that one, it's your back foot that counts!' We worked out it was three years after the Law had been changed!

With more League cricket now being played, with its fully qualified officials, the old style umpires are becoming a distant, even fond,

109

memory. From my rag-bag of umpiring 'incidents', I still chuckle over two, which remain fresh over the years.

The first concerns my old friend Sam, the passionate enthusiast and ultimate non-cricketer I mentioned earlier, in connection with evening matches at East Brighton Park. Some years later, NALGO had arranged a Sunday game against Preston Nomads at Fulking and for them, very much a prestige fixture. The regular NALGO umpire was there on the day, and performed with authority up to tea, when his side was batting. He then declared he would be unable to stand after tea, due to a prior engagement.

The NALGO skipper was faced with the option of asking Sam, who'd gone along to watch, to take over, or the embarrassment of asking Nomads to provide a batsmen to do the honours. Fatefully he opted for Sam who, to be fair, did not profess any skill or previous experience.

For the first over, Sam was led to the square leg position by a fielder, and not required to take any action. But when the Nomads umpire called 'Over!' and strolled away from the other wicket, Sam stayed put, happy to chat to square leg. Aware of a potential problem, the fielder changed the conversation, making heavy hints about going to the wicket, while nudging Sam repeatedly in the back in an effort to move him forward.

Sam, a big man, remained rooted to the spot as the embarrassed NALGO team tried surreptitiously to persuade him to the wicket. Finally, with everyone waiting for the new over, the bowler was forced to call out:

'Sam, you're supposed to stand here by the stumps.'

In a tense silence, with everyone straining to hear, Sam's cheery response was:

'Oh that's all right; I can see quite well from here!'

My other favourite umpiring story is generated from the competitive days of League cricket. It happened in St. James's first season in the East Sussex League in '86, when the 2nd XI took over a strong side to play Stone Cross near Eastbourne.

Losing the toss and put into bat, we scored as fast as possible, making 202 for 7 declared in 44 overs, leaving plenty of time to bowl them out.

With everyone fired up for a win as Stone Cross lost early wickets, two lower order batsmen put together a stand, and we became desperate to break this, and finish off the match.

With tension running high and the Stone Cross umpire at the wicket, Max Page tossed up a gentle, dead straight, good length ball. The batsman, bursting with confidence, took the most horrendous cross batted heave, flinging his left leg a yard away to square, but leaving his right a few inches in front of the stumps. He missed by a mile and the ball brushed the side of his back pad, before deflecting to wicket-keeper Bruce Nunn.

The St. James's team erupted in a roared, ecstatic appeal, with L.B.W. in mind, absolutely certain it would be given. Brooking no nonsense, with firm shake of the head, the Stone Cross umpire responded with an emphatic, 'Not out!', adding by way of justification, 'and in any case, he hit it.'

Realising the implication of this, 'keeper Bruce Nunn, ball still in glove, raised it aloft and appealed again:

'Well, how was that then umpire, caught?'

Clearly fed up with all this pressure, the umpire's second response was swift and final:

'And that's not out either.'

By the time I'd finished playing regularly, the newly merged St. James's Montefiore C.C. had an embarrassment of umpiring riches, with four regular fully qualified performers. Barry Foreman, Bill Gunn, Malcolm Hunter and Graham Gardner, made up a squad that was at least three more than I'd been used to, and a far cry from the amateurish situation when I started.

Though these umpires featured in my cricket during the '80's, from the humorous angle, I treasure memories of earlier performers in the 'bad old days' of friendly cricket.

The St. James's umpire for the '70's was Bert Amor, a spritely man who stood for the Club through the difficult period before we found our own Ground. Bert was a sharp student of the Laws, fully qualified, but an intense worrier. Having given an L.B.W., he often became wracked with doubt, and would be seen later locked in debate with the individual concerned. After a few pints, the discussion would end with

Bert regretting his decision, and the batsman apologising for his leg having made contact with the ball.

The incident I always associate with Bert Amor, took place on a May Saturday one year in a First XI League match at Waterhall. A bitterly cold day, with wind sweeping down the valley, everyone huddled in the tea room, while the St. James's fielders ran and jumped about trying to generate some warmth.

Bert Amor was at the bowler's wicket, when the batsman pushed the ball towards extra cover, producing an urgent shout for a single from the non-striker. Sensing the possibility of a run out, Bert sprang round to position himself correctly, crouching hands on knees, a few yards back from the wicket square on the off side.

Cover fielder Derek Pickering also sensed a run-out, as the batsman was on the back foot, and seemed surprised by the call. Derek swooped on the ball and flicked out his lightning fast return from low level, which should have scythed into or across the bowlers stumps. Claiming later it was due to the cold, Derek released the ball – a rogue buzz in fact – and it flashed through the air to hit Bert Amor smack on the back of the head.

I watched horrified as Bert, by reflex action, raised his hands as if surrendering, tilted his head up and then seemed to freeze in that position for a second. He then toppled forward in slow motion, to splat onto the ground like the great Buster Keaton himself.

It was a dreadful moment when one's emotions are torn two ways; with the ball travelling at that speed he could have sustained a serious injury and, though unobserved, I felt constrained to keep a straight face. Yet the sight of Bert keeling forward like a cardboard cut-out, induced an uncontrollable guffaw of laughter.

He was unconscious for a couple of minutes but thankfully, with liberal use of a wet sponge, was able to resume his duties none the worse for wear.

Undoubtedly my favourite umpire was Vic Bartholomew, who stood for St. James's when I first started playing regularly in the '60's. At that time Vic was Secretary of the Brighton Hove and District Umpires Association which operated a panel to serve the local clubs. For reasons I never understood, Vic attached himself to St. James's and became our regular umpire for the best part of ten years.

Vic was about five foot six tall, in his late fifties, with the traditional rotund shape of the immovable umpire. He conformed entirely to image and was typically taciturn, rarely volunteering a comment about anything. I believe also, he was a bit class conscious, feeling he was just a servant of the Club, obliged to know his place, and speak only if spoken to. This attitude was exacerbated at the time, as most of the players were extrovert 'chaps' from public school, whom I think he regarded as untrustworthy, and best left to their own foolish devices.

Behind the man was Mrs Bartholomew. No-one I knew had ever seen or spoken to her, yet she was held in some respect by her husband – someone who must be obeyed. I can't say she detested cricket, but she certainly wanted nothing to do with it, and the fact that Vic only stood on Saturdays, may have had something to do with her.

As an umpire I felt he was quite competent, though he seemed detached and unemotional throughout a match. He would march from square leg to the wicket on auto-pilot, and be unmoved by almost anything that happened on the field, funny or otherwise. Most umpires get annoyed by lack of acknowledgements from the scorers, but Vic would signal a four all afternoon if necessary, rather than shout a sarcastic comment to the boundary.

At the wicket he stood with his left arm, holding his ball counter behind his back, while his right hand was thrust deep into his coat pocket. This arrangement never changed and if handed sweaters, would manoeuvre them round his shoulders to keep his arms free.

When it came to appeals he would turn them down with a simple 'Not out' and discouraged any further discussion or comment. If he gave an appeal he made up his mind quickly, drawing his right hand out of his pocket to chest height, holding his finger up for at most two seconds, then diving it back again. On many an occasion this caused some confusion at the other end, if the batsman had blinked or turned his head away, and Vic was strangely reluctant to repeat the exercise.

Although he was respected as an umpire, it was off the field that the 'misunderstandings' arose between Vic and the St. James's players. As a non-driver he had to be collected and ferried to the match and liked to get home as soon as possible after the game. Usually this could be arranged for home games, but problems arose when we ventured into mid Sussex for an away fixture. The form after a match was to go into the local pub for the evening session, as in those days most club pavilions were not equipped with a bar.

Socially, it could be argued that Vic was a man ahead of his time, a teetotaller, he didn't smoke and detested being in a smokey atmosphere. Perfectly acceptable as that was, it didn't help the cohesion of the Club when the rest of us wanted to jug it up all evening. A compromise was worked out, with the 'chaps' taking over the Saloon bar, while Vic sat huddled alone by an open window in the Public bar, clutching a small brown ale and a bag of crisps. To be fair, he didn't object to this for half an hour or so, but got distinctly tetchy when it stretched to the late evening.

The uneasy relationship between Vic Bartholomew and the players was brought to a head by a famous incident after a match at Findon one year. It was a warm mid-summer evening and both sides piled into a pub in Findon village after the match. Vic was set up with ale and crisps and ventured to sit outside in the back garden, while we set about our thrash in the Saloon bar.

It was nearing closing time before the session broke up, and everyone piled into cars to go home at the same time. It wasn't just terrible that they forgot Vic, it was unforgivable that no-one even thought about him, till reminded some days later.

Apparently what happened was that, unaware of his misfortune, he waited impatiently till closing time, eking out his brown ale, as the light faded. He then found out the bad news when the barman started to lock the back door, and assured him there was no-one else left on the premises.

Never known to have sworn, the odd expletive must, surely, have escaped his lips, but it's certain he had to set off on a brisk walk to catch the last bus into Worthing. That was followed by the stopping train to Brighton and, because the buses had by then finished, an expensive taxi ride to his house. He arrived around one o'clock on Sunday morning and, it's not difficult to imagine, Mrs Bartholomew lurking behind the front door with rolling pin or worse.

With what remained of the Sunday, Vic penned a letter to the Club Committee, couched in the most vitriolic terms he could muster. Not only was he resigning forthwith, but he demanded an apology for this most appalling behaviour, etc, etc.

When the Secretary received this missive he didn't know what to do with it because, the Committee only met about once a year. After phone calls to senior players, it was agreed the letter was too hot to leave unanswered, so an unofficial meeting was arranged in a pub a week later.

After lengthy deliberations, or by the fourth round, it was decided to send a reply to Vic containing an abject apology and refusal to accept his resignation. But also, in an unintended masterstroke, someone suggested they should send a small box of *Cadbury's Roses*, as a sweetener to the unseen Mrs Bartholomew.

Duly done, the status of the Club leapt from rock bottom to sky high in Mrs B.'s eyes, and also put her Victor's umpiring activities in a much more favourable light. His resignation was quickly forgotten, and for some weeks even the hint of a smile played around his lips. Not only that, I clearly recall sharing a lift to a match soon after this incident, when, out of the blue, he volunteered the comment:

'It looks like being a nice day!'

This induced a stunned silence for some seconds, as we communicated doubts to each other, as to whether he was feeling well.

It's clear from the scorebook that St. James's were short of batting, for their local derby against Rottingdean in September '64 at Stanmer Park. There'd been a fair amount of rain during the week so the pitch was soft, but drying, and though there was plenty of cloud cover, there was every prospect of a full game.

The match started twenty minutes late with St. James's batting first, and openers Derek Pickering and John Lewis fairly raced away putting on 70 in forty minutes, when they were both out. I went in at three and mucked about for twenty minutes, struggling to survive against Jack Goss. As his rabbit, I knew it was fatal to play back as the ball hurried through, so I started determined to push forward; but the first time I didn't, I was bowled.

Peter Beecheno came in next at four having, by necessity, been pushed up the order on the day. Given the rare opportunity of building an innings, he grabbed the chance, scoring 75 in just over the hour to enable us to declare at tea with 194 for 4.

In reply Rottingdean got off to a sound start, with George Wilby scoring 63, and by six-thirty they had reached 127 for 3, with real hope of reaching the target with an hour to go. Events then conspired to kill off their hopes in a dramatic way.

Firstly, the weather had changed for the worse with the ground covered by dense black cloud, threatening to open up at any moment. This, allied to the rapidly fading light, meant that play would have been suspended in anything other than club cricket.

The second factor was three deliveries from Peter Beecheno, which took full advantage of the prevailing conditions. Beecheno was into his twelfth over from the Church end, having conceded 29 runs, with Vic Bartholomew standing at the bowler's wicket. A chap called Pinkum was batting, went right back onto his stumps, and missed a straight ball which skidded through low. The unanimous appeal had an air of formality about it, and Vic cut his fingerwork time down to half a second.

Next to the crease was Derek Stenton who, though not a front line batsmen, was an experienced cricketer who knew the basics. To his first ball, he went neither forward nor back, and ended missing a good length delivery which hit his front leg, just above the knee-roll. The appeal was more restrained and tentative, as height seemed a problem, and there was some ill tempered muttering from the opposition when Vic obliged again.

Facing the third ball was Peter Ross, over six foot tall, an accomplished all-round sportsman and something of a 'star' batsman. Beech had not bothered much about altering his field for the possible hat-trick, but there was real tension as he shuffled up to the wicket. The ball was short, but Ross plonked his front leg well down the track, as if getting forward out of harm's way. He didn't seem concerned when he failed to make contact, allowing the ball to thump into his pad mid-way between ankle and knee. Fielding at square leg I could say with certainty, the ball wouldn't have passed over the stumps.

No-one said anything, and only Beecheno seemed to be considering an appeal. He finished his follow through on the off side then turned, crouching, legs apart, hands on knees, with just his head between the line of the wickets. In a superbly theatrical display, he then slowly swivelled his gaze backwards and forwards between the two sets of stumps.

This went on for an age, as Ross stood defiant and disinterested at the other end. As I anxiously watched Beecheno, the next step became inevitable, and for the first time in my career, I said a fervent prayer that an opposition batsman wouldn't be given out. As all heads were bowed and eyes downcast, Beecheno finally whispered:

'Well, I've got to ask umpire, how was that?'

Vic Bartholomew had long since made up his mind. His finger shot up instantly, to complete his hat-trick of L.B.W.'s, while Ross did something I'd never seen on a cricket field. He exploded.

In a fraction of a second he stood on his toes, arched his back, and whirled both arms around, hurling his bat five yards down the wicket. At the same time, he let out an ear piercing 'Aaaaargh', followed by a gaggle of four letter words, emitted simultaneously. He then stood for several seconds in shocked disbelief, while the rest of us waited, heads still bowed, in embarrassed silence. Finally, still slowly shaking his head, he retrieved his bat and trudged off, cocooned in an audible cloud of wrath.

There was open mutiny on the Rottingdean bench as the waiting players dicussed whether to abandon the match. Things were eventually calmed down, mostly due to the efforts of their skipper, who also apologised to the officials along the lines:

'The lads got a bit excited'.

Vic Bartholomew's letter to the Committee, not unexpected, went on at some length about ungentlemanly conduct and bringing the game into disrepute. He also stated he'd never been so insulted in his life, and unless he received a full and unreserved apology from Rottingdean, would have no alternative but to resign from the Club.

For the Committee, it was an impossible conundrum, as they knew Rottingdean were more likely to be looking for an apology from St. James's. I don't know how it was all sorted out in the end, but presumably, it wouldn't have done any harm to have sent Mrs Bartholomew another box of *Cadbury's Roses*!

CHAPTER 8

PUTTIE

My favourite cricket character, and a friend still, was James Puttington, who played for St. James's for about ten years from the mid '60's. A fine games all-rounder, he'd been captain of cricket and fives at school, and played rugger to a good club standard later on. Short and stocky, he was physically fearless, leading to some memorable, if painful, heroics on the field.

When I first saw him, mid-brown hair parted in conventional 'chaps' style, he always had a pipe clenched firmly between teeth, and spent much time fussing around with lighters and cleaning rods.

He'd joined the Club from Rottingdean, was a busy batchelor around 35, heavily involved in the local sporting scene and its administration. Naturally, as a sitting target, he was soon voted onto our Committee, where he was left to get on with the Secretarial donkey work for some years.

The reasons for my affection and respect for Puttie, can be split into three areas. He'd acquired all the mannerisms from a top public school education, he was the ultimate 'domestic' cricketer, and he could create humour by simply being himself.

I've always admired and enjoyed, the polish, self confidence and style, exuded by the 'chaps', but in Puttie's case it had gone too far, opening the door to merciless leg-pulling. He was not just unselfish but incapable of a selfish act, not just polite but ridiculously polite. All of which inevitably, meant others took advantage of him, though never denting his cheery good humour.

His manners were delightfully old fashioned; in conversation if he wanted to disagree he wouldn't interrupt, but hold up his hand, fingers upwards, palm towards speaker. With head to one side he'd appeal for the chance to speak by repeating, with growing insistance,'With respect, with respect', until allowed to express his views. Then when he did so, he'd slowly turn his hand round to the horizontal, palm up, as if proffering his thoughts.

If anything at all went wrong, which he felt might have been his fault, he would repeat profuse apologies, usually starting with; 'Dreadfully sorry old boy, but…'. If angry, four letter words were never used of course, but wound up by the hurly burly of repartee, he could become quite forceful with, for example: 'Bother me, I must say I think your behaviour leaves much to be desired.'

I first noticed Puttie, with multi-coloured cap, hooped sweater and the rest, in the changing room at Stanmer Park one day. But what focussed my attention were the contents of his battered, old brown, suitcase, which seemed to contain something for any emergency. As well as cricket kit, there were bandages, elastoplast, talcum powder and ointments, all mixed in with tobacco, pipes, cleaners and lighter fuel, a few basic hand tools, plus various household fittings thrown in.

On the field half an hour later, we had our formal man to man introduction. Both posted to backward short leg, I was the squarer when the batsman pulled a loose ball passed me. I swung round to watch it clear the boundary first bounce, when I was surprised to hear a thump on the ground in front of me. Puttie was lying there, having dived seconds late for the ball. He rolled over, looked up at me and said:

'Dreadfully sorry old boy; I was a bit late on that one. I don't believe we've met. My name's James Puttington'.

With that he extended his arm upwards and we shook hands.

Over the season, I worked out that Puttie was the perfect 'domestic' batsman. His basic flaw was an exaggerated backlift, which meant he was bowled, or leg before, if a ball hurried through or kept low. He also had a habit of leaving anything outside off stump, by jumping across into line, and squatting low with bat over shoulder. It was fine in theory, to a short ball on a hard pitch, but at Stanmer it invariably lead to some painful bruises. On one occasion, he managed to get hit with all six balls of an over.

Usually he batted mid-order, but was moved up if the wicket was fiery, where his fearless defensive technique could be best employed. But he tended to get bogged down too often, making the bowling look difficult, and unwilling to risk an attacking shot.

One time when we needed quick runs before tea, the watching batsmen were pacing about in desperation, as Puttie pushed stoutly down the line. Finally, someone shouted in exasperation; 'For chrissake Puttie, get on with it!' Stung by this, Puttie immediately launched a full scale assault, playing shots he'd not used for years. Repeatedly lifting the bowlers back over their heads, he reached 50 before the declaration, to the delight and amazement of his team mates.

There's a hatful of Puttie stories on and off the field, I collected over the years, for constant re-telling in the bar. Perhaps they're dated now, but as a tribute to a great character, I've jotted down my favourites.

There was the game at Horley, about 25 miles up the main A23 from Brighton, when Puttie's car was late, and we started fielding three short. The skipper was not amused, and much less so when the three players didn't appear till 50 minutes into the match. Furiously he demanded:

'Where the hell have you been, Puttie?'

'Dreadfully sorry skipper, spot of bother on the A23; I rolled the car over at a petrol station!'

There's no answer to that. The skipper opened his mouth and said nothing, it was the most original excuse he'd heard, and of course, Puttie would never tell a lie.

Apparently they were cruising up the road, when Puttie noticed the petrol station and decided to fill up. As he was then almost level with the entrance, it was all a bit too sharp for his Ford Popular. Turning left, they rolled right over once, back to upright, without any serious damage to car or occupants. In the days before seatbelts, the three must've been well shaken up, but no doubt Puttie soothed things with: 'Dreadfully sorry chaps, very remiss of me, a slight misjudgement of speed...'.

Another memorable accident was at Ashurst Wood one year, when we batted first on a dodgy wicket. The star batsmen soon got out, or got themselves out, leaving Puttie to lead a dogged middle order rearguard action. This he did with great courage, taking all manner of painful blows without flinching. Then he went to hook a quickish ball, and top edged into his left eye.

It was a sickening blow, and he collapsed to writhe around in genuine distress by the crease. As always, everyone rushed up to help, but no-one knew what to do, so we stood there making well meaning, but conflicting suggestions. His eye was swelling and closing as we watched, and use of a cold, wet towel made no difference.

Eventually, he got over the worst of the shock and lay still, composing himself enough to utter his first coherent words:

'Bother me gentlemen, I'm dreadfully sorry. I seem to be holding the game up, please carry on without me.'

We carried him off, and then to hospital where he stayed a night for observation. When the skipper visited him later, he was still apologising about his 'inconsiderate' occupation of the crease.

Puttie and barbed wire had a sort of mutual attraction, and two incidents on this theme spring to mind. There was the rotten trick played on him, during our Sunday match at Firle one year. We were in the field after tea, and the home side's batsmen were taking a rustic approach to run scoring. Concentrating on hitting huge sixes, the ball was frequently deposited deep into the woods opposite the pavilion. It was quite a chore retrieving the ball, so Puttie soon found himself posted to deep long-on, near the three stranded, barbed wire fence which marked the boundary.

When yet another big hit disappeared into the trees, we took a rest while Puttie was left to do the necessary. He re-appeared at the other side of the fence, lobbed the ball in, then started to squirm, face downwards, under the bottom wire strand. Mid-way under, Pickering and B-P called anxiously in unison: 'Hold it Puttie, you're hooked up. Don't move!'

They then crept back to their positions and the game continued, with two more balls bowled, as Puttie lay rigid, face down in the mud, waiting assistance. When he twigged he'd been had, Puttie was not amused – furious even – and let loose a burst of vitriol at the culprits along the lines:

'Bother me, with respect, that sort off infantile behaviour is not really on.'

My favourite Puttie memory, with full barbed wire involvement, was during a match at Hailsham, on a glorious August Sunday. We'd batted first and with a star studded side, had cruised to 220 for 3 declared at tea.

Our opening bowlers were also first team standard and we picked up wickets, but also pushed the home side well behind the clock. The point arrived when we needed to buy wickets with plenty of runs, so the skipper invited N.F.K.Wilson, nephew of the man who founded St. James's C.C. in 1898, to toss up his high altitude leg breaks. N.F.K. was then a respected elder statesman, and his field placing had to be taken seriously. Our skipper therefore, held earnest discussions with his bowler, while discreetly signalling with hands behind back, for everyone to get back on the boundary.

The first ball was totally mis-read by the batsman, no respecter of the flighted full toss, who thrashed it high towards long-off. Puttie at long-on, set off with great determination towards the flight path, which, unfortunately, meant passing in front of the canvas sight screen. In my mind's eye I can still see what happened next. At full speed his foot got hooked under the first guy rope, and remarkably, he performed a perfect cart-wheel across the front of the screen. His momentum was such he started the second wheel, when a foot got tangled up in the other guy rope, and he was brought to earth like a snared deer.

Puttie's heroics were anyway to no avail, as the ball sailed twenty yards over the boundary. The second delivery was similar; this time it sailed over Puttie's head into the trees behind, and again, a barbed wire fence had to be negotiated. Safely done on the way out, but having thrown the ball back, he got hopelessly enmeshed in the wire, making matters worse by writhing about. Forced to shout for assistance, with much mirth among his colleagues, the skipper had to order two players to go and sort him out.

With that kerfuffle over, we settled for the third ball. By now super confident, the batsman launched into another full bloodied heave, sending the ball high in the sky towards Puttie. From the moment of contact he crouched stock still, eyes fixed on the missile, as it homed down into his waiting hands. He held the catch perfectly, to whoops of delight from all; a triumph of cool nerve over adversity.

Off the field, as well as being the butt for humour of all sorts, Puttie provided great value in the bar, puffing away on his ever present pipe. After a session, having not eaten since tea, we would often arrange to stop at a Chinese or Indian restaurant on the way home. By the time we sat down it could be nearing eleven o'clock, and everyone ravenously hungry.

On one such occasion, ten of us piled into a Chinese, and decided to make one bulk order for everyone. Fine in theory, but the selection process got bogged down with individual likes and dislikes, so, as it dragged on, Puttie came to the rescue:

'Er, ladies and gentlemen, could I assist by suggesting a very nourishing, balanced meal, details of which I always carry in my diary? I can adjust quantities to suit.'

By then happy to delegate the task, we agreed and left him to get on with it. When the waiters arrived they gave us some funny looks, as they served up mounds of fried rice, pilau rice, plain rice, bamboo shoots and mixed vegetables, and nothing much else.

Apparently, Puttie had ordered from a list of numbers, which he thought were universal to all Chinese restaurants.

Then there was the time we stopped in the High Street in Lewes, on the way back from a game at Maresfield. There were seven of us at one table, and we decided to order one main dish each, which would be shared out all round. This was fine, but as the dishes were passed round, because of the seating arrangements, Puttie got the last portion in each case.

Trying to spoon out one seventh from an oval dish was not easy, everyone, naturally tending to err on the generous side. As a result, Puttie's plate had only two dozen grains of rice, six peas and one prawn ball, rolling about on it, when we'd finished serving up.

When his attention was drawn to the discrepancy, Puttie's immediate response was:

'Perfectly alright old boy; I wasn't that hungry anyway.'

If that wasn't bad enough, at the end of the meal, someone asked Puttie for a loan to help settle the bill.

There's many more Puttie stories, like the day he was obliged to wear someone else's flannels, with hilarious result, or the time he went into the showers smoking his pipe upside down, with painful result.

When I wrote 'The Domestic Cricketer', there was plenty of humorous material to write a chapter on my comic hero, so I did just that. Having finished, I sat back to review my efforts and decided I'd been a bit unfair, and merciless with my ribbing. I'd never seen him at his sporting best, and by emphasising the foul-ups of his 'domestic' years, had made him out to be something of a twit. In the serious sense of course, this was not true, so I resolved to clear the air by arranging a heart to heart chat, before anything was published.

In the nature of things it didn't happen. There was quite a lot to be organised in the last few weeks and Puttie, recently married, had moved from the area and taken a job overseas, or so I'd heard. These are the lame excuses of a coward, but my conscience was such, as soon as copies were available, I sent a signed one, with a friendly note, to where I thought he was living.

Uncharacteristically I got no reply, but assumed it never got to him, so I didn't worry about it and we lost touch. He returned to live in Croydon in the '80's but made no contact, so a new hobby of 'Puttie sightings' developed, when people reported they'd seen him somewhere.

For my fiftieth birthday party in August '90, I made a determined effort to track him down, and duly done, he readily agreed to put in an appearance. It was a super do, with lots of my cricketing pals there, but with so much going on, it wasn't the right time to mention my book. A few months later, we received an invitation to dinner one Saturday from his wife Marion, which I thought might be the perfect opportunity to broach the subject.

On the day, when we arrived we were introduced to teenage son David, shown the house, had cocktails, and said all the usual polite things, before going into the dining room for the meal. The table was relatively small, but laid out with all the trimmings, including the most enormous wine glasses, about a foot tall and holding half a pint at least. Carol and I sat one side, David the other, with Puttie and Marion at opposite ends

Puttie busied himself pouring out a rich red wine, as we continued the general chit-chat. When he'd sat down Carol launched into a story, which she ended dramatically by sweeping her hand across the table in his direction. Unhappily, a finger caught in the top of her glass and its contents were flung, at waist level, over our host.

It's difficult to believe the results could have been more disastrous. Puttie was wearing a white shirt and light oatmeal summer slacks; these were soaked from waist to knee. The table cloth was saturated for about a square yard, and a sizeable red stain was growing on the bright gold carpet.

My policy in these situations is to say and do nothing, letting everyone else flap about. I sat back and listened as Carol, on hands and knees with napkin, frantically tried to stop the spread of wine on the carpet, while issuing a string of abject apologies. Marion calmly debated with herself, whether it would be necessary to change the tablecloth and start again. And Puttie of course, as a perfect gentleman, stood there saying all the right things.

He came out with three gems in not many more seconds. For the wine: 'There's plenty more where that came from.' For his trousers: 'I never did like that colour.' And for the carpet: 'It's about time we had a new one anyway.'

Trauma over, we enjoyed a fine meal, but it was not till much later, when our wives had gone outside, that Puttie and I found ourselves alone. Tentatively I broached the subject of my book, and the following considered, tense conversation took place:

'Puttie, er; just as a matter of interest, did you ever get the copy of my book I sent you in '77?'

'Yes I did.'

'Oh fine, umm, only I didn't hear from you, so I wondered if I'd sent it to the right place.'

'Oh yes, sorry. That was very remiss of me, I should have written to thank you.'

'Well it doesn't matter now. But I just wondered if you had any comments to make?'

'It was excellent. Very good indeed.'

'Well thank you very much Puttie, its nice of you to say so. But were you happy with everything…'

'Oh yes Dick, the content and literary style were absolutely first rate.'

'Thanks again Puttie. I er… I just really wanted to reassure myself that nothing I'd written had caused you any offence?'

'No not really…'

'Well, you imply there might have been something…'

'No no; it's nothing of any great importance.'

'Well look Puttie, it was a bit of fun, just a mickey take. The last thing I wanted to do was upset you in any way.'

'Oh yes I realised that but, not to put too fine point on it, there was one aspect I was not entirely happy about.'

'Well come on Puttie, we're old mates; what was the problem?'

'Well er…and I don't want you to take this the wrong way old boy. But with respect, I just thought you made me out to be a bit of a twit!'

My eyes swivelled to closely study the ceiling. For several seconds, I fought to fashion a suitable reply, but nothing came. So I chickened out:

'Well Puttie, it's been a delightful evening. I think it's about time we made a move.'

CHAPTER 9

THE DREADED INVITE

My father, a proud Vice-President of St. James's, took me to my first cricket club dinner when I was 20, before becoming a regular Club member. Held shortly before the new season at the Pavilion Hotel Brighton, the all-male 'Stag' Dinner was the main social event of the close season, eagerly anticipated by all.

Knowing few of the diners, I was a shade apprehensive about the affair, half expecting to get embroiled in some secret initiation rites. Nevertheless, smart and scrubbed with Club ties and dark lounge suits, we arrived at the required 'seven thirty for eight', on our best behaviour.

The layout of the Crown Room, with top table across the far end and three branches at right angles, was an arrangement I now know to be standard for these occasions. Places were set for about sixty diners, and at the other end was a small, temporary bar, formed from trestle tables, a couple of barrels, some bottles of spirits, and dozens of glasses.

I was instantly attracted to the cosy ambience of the room, assisted by the ornate candelabra and subdued wall lighting. When we arrived there were twenty diners already there, pints in hand, split into groups each locked in animated conversation.

Coming out of cricketing hibernation, they were renewing acquaintances, reminiscing about last season and debating prospects for the new. As more people arrived they would make straight for the bar, but, with only one waiter on duty, it was impossible to get a drink quickly, a situation unaltered over the years.

The sense of cameraderie and warmth was enhanced by the actual temperature, which increased steadily as events unfolded. With smoking more prevalent then, and in the absence of any ventilation, let alone air-conditioning, everyone was soon enveloped in a bluish haze, as the temperature climbed into the eighties. As the evening wore on, eyes would sting and collars have to be loosened, but removing jackets was considered 'bad form'. (The fug got so bad one year I remember the President halting proceedings, and instructing someone to: 'Open all available windows!')

By quarter past eight there was a dense crowd round the bar, who looked as if they'd be quite happy to stay there all evening. The Toastmaster's first plea for diners to take their places was ignored, but two or three shouts later, backed up with some physical persuasion, everyone was shepherded into their seats. The President then said 'grace', and the meal began with the hub-bub quickly back to its earlier level.

A tradition of St. James's Dinners was the regular calling of toasts, expressing due thanks for work done for the Club or, more frequently, subjecting some poor soul to ridicule. A typical mocking toast would be, say: 'The President would like to take wine with that smooth, dashing, free-scoring, left-handed opening batsman, who brilliantly contrived to put together four successive ducks last season.'

The first, formal part of the dinner started with a four course meal, spread over an hour and a half, with waitresses struggling to get between tables, a few diners wandering about, and the noisy chatter only halted at intervals by the Toastmaster. Around coffee time, he announced a ten minute interval, after which, relieved and with glasses recharged, diners re-seated for the second half, ready for the introduction of the first of four speakers.

Speeches averaged ten to fifteen minutes, and I realised immediately, considerable expertise and experience were needed to be successful. There were serious comments and thanks to individuals, but for the most part, speeches were based on a mix of cricket stories, nostalgia and humour. This was spiced up with witticisms, asides and fresh jokes, plus an element of repartee with the audience.

It was nearly eleven o'clock before the last speaker sat down at my first Dinner, the whole occasion having a laid-back and timeless air. I certainly found it fascinating and enjoyable, even if the time spent sitting in the hot, smoky atmosphere, tested my stamina.

Over the years I became hooked by the ritual of cricket club dinners, especially the relaxed, if not lacksadaisical, approach to the organisational side. Typical form was no-one seemed certain if the right number of meals had been ordered, who was supposed to be there, and who had actually turned up. This would create a mini-drama, as the organiser, with furrowed brow, scurried around with pencil and paper, trying to share sixty meals between sixty two diners. I also developed a healthy respect, verging on awe, for those courageous enough to speak. The daunting list of skills required, may be possessed by professional speakers, but for many club members, being pressed to perform, it was an ordeal they weren't willing to face. As well as the prepared part of the speech, the best speakers would indulge in impromptu repartee with prominent members of the audience, often much funnier than the formal part. And of course, the skilled performers would closely monitor the mood of the audience, adapting their speech accordingly. On the other hand, some would simply dive in and reel off a string of blue jokes, oblivious to any embarrassment caused.

I considered Jack Smith to be one of the best speakers in the early '60's. His technique was to tell a shaggy dog story while flinging out insults and asides, and encouraging repartee as he went along. His 'charisma' was such that he'd command rapt attention, his audience keen to catch every word. All this would string out the story indefinitely, so that he'd sometimes never reach, or forget the punch line, but still leave everyone weak with laughter.

The pitfalls awaiting were just as obvious; the audience may be bored, restless, talkative, even hostile, and that was before he got to his feet. Then one had to cope with people wondering about, talking among themselves, waitresses dropping plates, and every kind of interruption.

With this in mind, it was with naive optimism, that I toyed with the idea of building a speaking career. I should've stayed on the safe side of the fence, but in '65 I volunteered to propose the health of the guests at the St. James's Dinner that year. I've often puzzled over my real motive since, and, apart from masochism, I suspect it was to crawl to the Club's hierarchy, at a time when my performances on the field 'left much to be desired'.

In the weeks before the Dinner, I worked feverishly on my speech, constantly revising the stories, trying to create a polished professional effort that would bring the house down. As the big day drew near, my brain - such as it is - went into overdrive, obsessed with every detail and leaving nothing to chance.

At the start of the Dinner, I went through the pre-speeches ritual with fixed smile and half-hearted effort to appear relaxed, while inside I felt queasy with nerves, or more accurately, fear. Eating the meal I learnt my first lesson; because of my frightened state, all drinks tasted like warm water and all food like cardboard. This of course, devalued the idea of 'singing for your supper', as it would have have been more enjoyable to stay at home with a piece of stale bread and margarine.

Such was my mental torment as the moment approached, I was passed caring by the time the Toastmaster finished his introduction, just glad of the chance to get on with it. Barely pausing to take breath, I ploughed straight into my prepared text, vaguely aware I was being listened to, and slowing or stopping the flow of words only for scheduled laughter. Galloping to the finishing line, it was with overwhelming relief that I reached the formal toast at the end, and sank back onto my chair exhausted.

Surprisingly, my effort was well received, with most stories accorded laughter or at least mild amusement. All in all, I felt I'd given value for money, but in my review of the event, there were lessons to be learned, especially one disaster still etched on my mind.

My first error was that, in my state of nerves, I hadn't bothered to listen to the preceeding speakers. This meant I'd ignored compliments which should have been acknowledged, but also failed to fling back with interest, various subtle digs. Generally, I hadn't assessed audience reaction, adjusted my speed, attempted off the cuff comment, or reacted to any repartee.

But the real lesson came when I was halfway through my text, and had launched into a long tale taking the mickey out of Puttie. In the preamble, I was earnestly detailing events after a match, when I said: '...and I approached Puttie, while in the showers, with soap in hand...'.

The shrieks and gales of laughter that greeted this line, stopped me dead in my tracks. After the initial shock, I stood there stunned and bemused, my mind racing about trying to work out why they were laughing and, more to the point, what I should do next. By the time the commotion had subsided I was none the wiser, so I carried on lamely, my punch line being received in near silence by an audience no longer interested.

It's ironic to reflect now; that line generated more uncontrolled laughter than anything I've ever said since. It all stemmed from my youthful innocence; though I'd read all the fuss about the Wolfenden Report on homosexuality, I'd never studied the mechanics of the subject.

Thus launched on my speaking career, word of my availability spread by jungle telegraph, and I was determined to improve my performance next time out. My second speech was at the Preston Nomads Annual Dinner, where I was invited to propose the health of the Club. Again I busied myself in detailed preparation, weaving in double entendre's, innuendo's and asides, around the leading Nomads players, whom I knew quite well.

More relaxed this time, I read my text with a clear, positive delivery, but became aware after a few minutes, that it was being received in near silence. Desperate for laughs, I increased my pace in the hope they would find something less boring. Gabbling away I soon ran out of material, came to the formal toast, and sat down. To my surprise, the applause was much stronger than I'd expected, and opinion was I'd made a witty and amusing speech.

On reflection, I reckoned I'd made several errors, mainly by being too clever by half, many of the innuendo's and witticisms passing the audience by. Then, because I'd constructed complex double entendre's, it took a fair time for the sharpest listener to unravel the meaning, funny or not. And again, by delivering my lines too fast, everyone was obliged to concentrate like mad, to stand a chance of understanding it.

It was around this period that a certain Jim Bebbington joined St. James's from Shoreham and was destined to play a pivotal, and terminal, role in my speaking career. A tall gangling off-spinner, he bowled accurately and flat, with a well disguised, flighted slower ball, and could plug away for long spells. Impressive though this was, his personality, infectious sense of humour and, arguably, the sharpest line in repartee I've come across, fascinated me. It was guaranteed that anyone unwise enough to engage him in verbal combat, came off second best, and quickly.

After a couple of years with St. James's, Bebbington got a new job in the Cotswolds area, moved house and was not seen, or heard of, for some years. Just before he went I asked him why he was going:

'U.K. Sales Manager, two litre Granada and lots more £K. I'd've been a fool to turn it down.'

His legacy to the Club was his stunningly simple method of financial control, something I've always regretted I didn't think of earlier. Whenever he played a match, he arrived at the ground with exactly thirty shillings in cash on him. In those days, that amount was just enough to cover the match fee, tea money and a half of bitter afterwards. So when he'd spent his thirty bob, it was left to others to decide whether he would be left wandering about the bar, with empty glass in hand.

My speaking career continued ingloriously, as I painfully gained experience, and picked up more skills of the subject. I abandoned using a detailed prepared text, as this allowed a more natural dialogue, and the possibility of repartee with the audience. I was beginning to be confident enough to think on my feet, and ready to counter comment from any quarter.

Of course, there's always a trap for the unwary. On one occasion, I flung back a deft riposte to a comment, and as laughter ensued, I waited quietly relishing my triumph. When it was time to continue, not only had I forgotten the story I was telling, but couldn't find the place in my notes to remind me. I stood there, red faced, desperately shuffling papers for an age, before I was able to continue.

After years of evolution, my technique for a typical stag cricket dinner was to draw up a list of stories, or anecdotes, in sequence, as a basic memory jogger. I would then try to tell each story as if I was in a crowded bar after a match, anxious to keep everyone's attention. On the whole this worked well enough, though it did little to reduce my chronic pre-speech nerves.

Having sorted that out, a new problem arose; how to find suitable material. I've always believed a speaker at a cricket dinner should tell cricket related stories, or anecdotes about cricketers. I've also found it embarrassing and potentially boring to keep repeating the same material. Fortunately, my fund of stories was swollen by our humorous construction of the 'domestic cricketer', a concept that could be readily appreciated by other club players.

Whenever I got depressed about the hazards of after-dinner speaking, I'd reminded myself of the Brunswick Dinner at the Dudley Hotel each year, which I attended as a guest. Very much an up-market occasion, I envied and marvelled at the confidence and gravitas of the six speakers, who usually commanded rapt attention and were often very funny.

However, the Brunswick Dinner highlighted yet another hazard for the unsuspecting speaker, the brilliant Toastmaster. Tony Dougal, who did the job for many years, certainly came into that category. He used to sit opposite the top table and, with liberal use of a large gavel, dominated affairs throughout. Some of his introductions would last several minutes, and totally up-stage the person waiting to speak.

He told the best jokes I've heard at a cricket dinner, always fresh, often highly topical, and I believe, carefully rehearsed. Having won attention, he would wait for complete silence before launching into a story with a clear, slow delivery. He would employ many 'ers' and 'umm's' as a deliberate affectation to emphasise his words, plus a mock seriousness to reinforce the humour.

Taking stock of my own 'career', by the mid-'70's my enthusiasm to win renown as a top class speaker was beginning to wane. Increasingly shell shocked with pre-speech nerves, I was becoming bogged down, obsessed even, with the hazards and complexities of it all.

I envied the professional cricketers and 'star' celebrities, who could dip into their fund of stories, apparently without preparation, week in week out, to a usually appreciative audience. These speakers of course, had the massive advantage that their sporting exploits are already known, and all club players are fascinated, by snippets of inside gossip from the top game.

Another development around that time further demoralised me; clubs started moving away from the stag dinner towards a mixed event. Though I had no objection in principle, this meant half the audience were probably uninterested in cricket, or gained their rudimentary knowledge under sufferance. As most of my material was based on events on field, or around personalities, all of this would mean next to nothing to the female audience. I reckoned therefore, apart from the 'domestics', my material was useless as far as mixed dinners were concerned.

When 'The Domestic Cricketer' was published in '77 I felt an obligation to the publisher, to make myself available as a speaker, on the theory it might assist sales. I reluctantly accepted therefore, an invitation to speak at the Southwick C.C. Annual Dinner, with Carol, at a restaurant on Hove seafront. The format I understood, was to be a four course meal, followed by speeches, and then dancing for the rest of the evening.

For once I didn't worry too much about my speech, knowing I could use the 'domestics' Memo as the basis. With a few general comments thrown in, and appropriate thanks to the Club, I reckoned I could get away with it, and justify our free tickets.

On the day, Carol and I were met by our hosts, plied with drinks in the Bar till dinner time, then ushered to pole position on the top table. When we'd sat down, I had my first chance to study the diners and, with no disrespect to Southwick, I was dismayed by what I saw. It was in fact a family occasion, with children in attendance as well as the womenfolk, ages ranging down to twelve. From that moment I felt utterly defeated, and, even if capable, didn't have the wit or resolve to change my speech in the time available.

Having suffered the cardboard and warm water routine, I got up for my speech, with a fatalistic, couldn't care less, attitude. Rattling through the 'Memo', I kept a wary eye on the twelve year old to see if he'd slump unconscious on the table. At the end, I sat down down to what seemed warm and genuine applause, and a quick glance at the young lad showed him joining in, though he may have been under orders.

With much soul-searching after this event, I decided in principle to turn down future invitations to speak. The constant search for new material, the agonies of the drafting process, the numbing pre-speech nerves, and the sheer stress of the speech itself, were simply too much for me. As an unpaid performer, I felt I'd made my contribution to the club game, and could bow out after an honourable effort.

Having made this irrevocable decision, a chance meeting in the spring of '77, was to lead to one of the most traumatic events of my life. I was hurrying through the crowded shopping precinct in Tunbridge Wells one Saturday morning, when I got into a left, right, left, tango, with a tall man, as I tried to dodge into a shop entrance. About to go for the Ali double shuffle, I looked up to find my opponent was none other than the long departed Jim Bebbington.

It must have been seven years since I'd seen him, and after ecstatic greetings we got down to sketching in the intervening period. Apparently, he'd moved two years earlier to live near Tunbridge Wells, and was commuting to London from there. His reasons, unsurprisingly, were: 'Sales Director, Volvo Estate and a lot more £K. I'd 'ave been a fool to turn it down.'

Cricketwise, he was still playing regularly, had joined Rusthall C.C. and was already a leading light on their Committee.

In reply, I said nothing so dramatic had happened in my little world, and, searching for something of interest to say, added casually to avoid appearing smug:

'Oh there's is one thing; I'm just about to get a book published....'.

His instant reply was:

'Oh are you. I'm on my fifth actually, old boy!'.

There's not a lot you can say to that, so I was effortlessly done off once again. We finished the conversation with a vague promise to make contact, and that was that for the time being.

Six months later, I got a phone call one evening from Bebbington, which, from its up beat tone, I could tell was likely to end in a dreaded invitation to speak at a cricket club dinner. I was right, and when the moment arrived, launched into my standard spiel about having retired and so on. As a salesman, Bebbington took this initial set-back as a challenge, and appealed to my vanity by suggesting I'd be able to sell dozens of copies of my new book, having shamelessly plugged the thing during my speech.

Inevitably, I succumbed to this flannel, and agreed in principle to do the speech the following January. He said he'd phone in December to make final arrangements, and in an apparently casual afterthought, just before putting the receiver down, added: 'Oh by the way, I've moved to Newton Abbot.'

With my parochial outlook, I assumed he'd changed clubs and there was one called Newton Abbot the other side of Tunbridge Wells. When it dawned on me he meant the town 200 miles away in the west country, I could only shake my head in disbelief. The whole thing was so ridiculous, I felt my only obligation was to dream up a plausible excuse, in time for the next phone call.

It turned out to be easier than expected. Looking at the details and cost of the trip, I reckoned the train fare, an overnight stay, and incidentals, would work out between £50 and £70. Truthfully, my excuse would be I couldn't afford it, and with that in mind, I didn't worry any more about it.

When the December phone call came, I started the chat in buoyant mood by asking about his sudden move to Newton Abbot:

'Managing Director Designate, a B.M.W., a lot more £K. I'd 'ave been a fool to turn it down.'

We continued in this confident style until we reached the nitty-gritty, and he asked if I was O.K. for the dinner.

Switching to a more conspiratorial tone; I said there was nothing more I fancied than a cricket dinner in the West Country, a comfortable train ride along the scenic coastal route, enjoying the winter delights of Devon and Dorset, an appetising meal with an old chum, and an overnight stay at a charming country hotel. This bullshit rolled effortlessly off the tongue, and he listened intently till I got to the punch line. With abject apologies and great regret, I said I couldn't make it because I simply couldn't afford the £50 to £70 cost of the trip.

As soon as he got my drift, he took over the conversation and reeled off a string of statistics about South Devon C.C.: five cricket teams, three hockey teams, squash courts, clubhouse with restaurant open year round, and annual turnover more than ten thousand pounds. Put in that context therefore, paying my expenses would be peanuts and present no problem at all!

Having comprehensively shot myself in both feet, I put the phone down, after finalising arrangements, resigned to the fact there was no way of avoiding the trip. I sat glumly contemplating the prospect, nagging worry about what I could say adding to my woes. As everyone except Bebbington would be a stranger, I decided the only speech I could do would be the 'Memo' from my book, which I could make last about ten minutes.

It was a bitter January Friday, when I left at mid-day for the fateful journey which involved: driving to Tunbridge Wells station, train to Charing Cross, underground to Paddington and 'Inter-City' to Newton Abbott. It was freezing cold, not noticeably scenic, getting dark from the halfway stage, and there was a sprinkling of snow on the ground. Bebbington met me off the train at six-thirty, and drove me to the White Hart Hotel in the town centre. In my pocket I'd kept the receipts of my expenses, and after a struggle with my conscience, decided it not unreasonable to include the sandwich and coffee I'd bought en route.

Entering the hotel, I was pleased to find the layout and ambience similar to the Pavilion in Brighton, with bar already full of grey suited diners, pints in hand. Bebbington introduced me to one or two, apparently at random, then disappeared into the throng. If not actually in charge, he seemed to be a major player, something I found surprising as he'd only been there a few months.

I was then passed a message that the Club Treasurer would 'like a word', which could only mean one thing, my expenses. My final costs were less than estimated, as Bebbington was putting me up for the night. Nevertheless, I felt uncomfortable, even furtive, as I was introduced to the Treasurer. After a few pleasantries he said, as he pulled out a cheque book:

'I believe you've got some 'expenses?'

Embarrassed I stammered something like:

'Well er,...actually, I'm afraid it comes to er...£33-78p – I've got all the receipts.'

Without hesitation he said, 'let's call it £34', and busied himself with filling in the cheque carefully noting the spelling of my name. With a flourish he then put it in his pocket saying: 'Fine. If you see me after dinner the cheque will be ready for you'. That hurt.

When dinner was announced, we filed into the main room set for around eighty. Bebbington led me to the top table, which had a lower ceiling than the main area, seats along one side only, and rather dimly lit. Unusually, the other tables ran parallel, with a gangway in the centre at right angles from the middle of the top table.

Bebbington and I seemed to be in the most important positions in the centre, with no sign of a President or Chairman. To my surprise, he told me he was making the third speech, and I would be replying, last, on behalf of the guests. I soon began to feel hot, stuffy and uncomfortable, as the temperature rose in the alcove, plus the usual pre-speech nerves.

After the interval the Toastmaster introduced the first speaker, thankfully without jokes or too much fuss. He was in his late twenties, well armed with cue cards, each with an in-joke tailored to a prominent Club member. They were witty and original, an ideal way of starting the entertainment, and well received by the audience.

Next on was a hospital consultant, about forty-five, a thoroughbred 'chap', complete with starched collar and slicked down, parted hair. He exuded confidence, taking immediate control of affairs, and reeled off a catalogue of misfortunes that had befallen patients in the operating theatre, most of which were greeted with hearty laughter.

It wasn't really to my taste, but when he quoted that there were an average of twelve men per month, admitted to U.K. hospitals for emergency treatment, because their private parts had got enmeshed in the zips of their trousers; I found myself wincing rather than laughing. Nevertheless, the speech was highly polished and professionally delivered, and much appreciated by the fully warmed up audience.

The Toastmaster then introduced Bebbington as the third speaker, in theory, to toast the health of the guests. Rising to his feet, he tossed out a couple of witty asides, before launching into his speech with undisguised gusto.

For the next twenty minutes he regaled the audience with the whole gamut of jokes, repartee, stories and banter in a relentless quick-fire barrage. He moved effortlessly from American to South African to Australian to Irish jokes, all with perfect accents, in a global *tour de force* of humour.

It was the funniest speech of its type I'd ever heard, and the audience were carried along with it all the way. People were banging the table with their fists, rocking back in their chairs and literally falling about with laughter, as I sat impassively next to him. I could feel my face getting dry and taut, as that slow queasy churning in the stomach started, a feeling I had only previously experienced before important soccer matches. To put it mildly, I was becoming distinctly uncomfortable, conscious of the fact I was the only person not enjoying himself.

Unbelievably, the last joke in his speech, greeted with hysterical laughter, was:

'They say the old ones are the best ones. Who was that lady I saw you with last night? That was no lady that was my wife!'

The ecstatic applause took several minutes to die down, and several more for the audience to wipe tears from their eyes and compose themselves.

During this time, my misery notwithstanding, I focussed my attention on one chap in a gangway seat in front of me. He seemed so overcome with exhaustion, he'd finished up slumped at an angle across his chair, head lolling to the right on his chest, and left arm dangling lifeless in the gangway. Had he died laughing?

As I sat there in abject dismay, feigning the occasional smile for the sake of appearances, I was also subjected to a form of water torture to add to my discomfort. Just behind my head was a small extractor fan in the outside wall, which was working the wrong way round. Sweat on my skull was running down the rats-tails at the back of my neck, and the beads formed cooled to near freezing by the jet of icy air, before dropping down inside my collar.

The saying, 'beam me up Scottie', was totally inadequate to express my feelings as I sat there dejectedly awaiting my fate. More truthfully, I prayed for release with a passion and fervour I've never achieved before or since. As I awaited my introduction, it was not just the nadir of my speaking career, but, arguably, the nadir of my whole life.

My body seemed to become frozen with fear, increasing dramatically, as the Toastmaster got to his feet for the introduction. Further agonies were added, by welcoming me fulsomely as, 'a cricket writer' and 'well known in Sussex cricket'. By the time he'd finished I was in a state of utter despair, my body paralysed with fear.

But I knew it was time to stand up, so my brain started yelling at my body to do this, but paralysis had set in and I was unable to move. For several seconds, I had to psyche myself up, by screaming internal commands like: 'get up you coward!', 'bounce up and grab the mike', 'be positive' and 'attack, attack', in order to initiate some movement.

When at last the signal got through, unhappily, it bypassed my torso and activated my calf muscles, sending knees, lower legs and feet rocketing upwards. Hit by this fast moving mass, my body was pitched forwards and upwards, towards the edge of the table. I just managed to manoeuvre my elbows onto the top, so I could then lever myself shakily upright.

But there were more agonies; during the frenetic juxtaposition of forces in my body during this movement, my head must have flicked backwards as a reaction. A bead of salty sweat was tossed off my eyebrow to fall back into the centre of my right eyeball. This not only stung but, I was also temporarily blinded.

To the audience, I must have looked like a frightened rabbit trapped in car headlights, and I have no recollection of what happened till the end of my speech. I can only remember the man with the dangling arm, steadily winch himself up right, reaching the vertical as I finished.

To my surprise and great relief, the applause was quite warm, if restrained, and they clearly appreciated the concept of 'domesticity'. As the formal part of the dinner was wound up, I tried to compose myself after my ordeal, and allow my nervous system to recover. Nothing seemed to have been permanently damaged, and my priorities were still in order; I set off to find the Treasurer to collect my expenses cheque.

This done and armed with a pint, I mingled in the Bar, determined to find out what I'd done and said during my speech. I listened to the usual polite comments: 'well done', 'just what the occasion called for', 'extremely amusing' and 'most interesting', which revealed nothing below the surface. Becoming more determined to find the truth, I picked on a studious young chap who'd said, 'a most interesting concept', and tried to dig deeper. From talking about 'domesticity', I manoeuvred the chat round to the style of my delivery which, he finally and reluctantly admitted was, 'a bit strange'.

Verbally gripping him by the tie, I eventually forced him to reveal the vital clue to what had happened.

'Well if you insist,…' he said, '…and I don't want to cause you any offence, but actually, you sounded as if you were delivering the sermon in church!'

I laughed inwardly and relaxed when I heard this, everything falling into place. My brain, frozen with fear, had switched to auto-pilot and I'd read the 'Memo' with a solemn po-faced expression. Luckily, the audience exhausted from Bebbington's barn-storming speech, weren't capable of further raucous laughter. The tempo of my speech, with its gently amusing idea of 'domesticity', had perfectly matched the needs of the moment. It was just about the only thing I could put on the positive side of the balance sheet.

On my journey home the next day, I was light headed, demob happy even, at the realisation I'd be making no more after-dinner speeches. I could claim I'd tried hard, made a contribution to the game etcetera etcetera, but the skill and talent needed were beyond me. I've also never changed my view that to be a successful after dinner speaker, is just about the most difficult task in the game.

Since then, I've sat back to enjoy the efforts of others, my sympathies on their side, as someone who's been there and failed.

CHAPTER 10

ST. BEES TOUR

Having played together for St. James's for some years, many of my generation had become firm friends off the field, and the possibility of a Club tour was touted around in the late '60's. Various false starts were made, and it really needed an enthusiastic contact the other end, somewhere, to arrange fixtures and get the ball rolling. When this eventually happened, it led to the Club's first full scale tour, and a delightful chapter in my cricket career.

David Marshall, who played for the Club for a few seasons, got a job as a Housemaster at St. Bees School in Cumbria. After he'd settled in, he invited St. James's to send up a team for the Bank holiday weekend at the end of May '73. Two all-day matches were to be played, both on the School ground, against the Ist XI on the Saturday, and his own Select XI on the Sunday.

From the practical angle, travelling over 400 miles each way for two games of cricket was a drawback, but the advantage was we'd be put up free in School dormitories or staff houses. This kept the overall cost down, petrol, food and kitty money being the major items.

For the first trip we travelled up Friday afternoon, conveniently arriving around opening time, allowing us to check out the local hostelries that evening. Then we played the School First XI in an all-day match, before attending a sumptuous buffet supper laid on in the Dining Room. After the Sunday match, another convivial session set things up for the trip home on the holiday Monday. 12 players went on that trip and I immediately established a record by not playing at all; I was not selected for the Saturday, then too ill to play on Sunday!

The Tour was a great success, and a repeat invitation was received from the School for the following year. It was thought a good idea, and make the travelling more worthwhile, to fit in an evening match at Eskdale. In the subsequent year the same thinking applied, and an afternoon match against Cockermouth was added. Then again, for the next trip, it was difficult to refuse an invitation for a game at Gosforth. So the Tour grew, with the commencing date creeping forward, such that in the final format the first match started at 6.00 Wednesday evening.

For the sake of appearances with our womenfolk, the Tour was always called, 'just a long weekend'. This description became more far-fetched when later on, some of the keen golfers went up on the Monday, to get in a few pre-cricket rounds. But, as the Tour was strictly male only, and constantly subject to feminine disapproval, this shallow pretence was important.

After a few years, there were found to be a number of unforeseen advantages to the venue for the Tour. It was a long way from London, and, psychologically, this seemed to relax everyone, as the pace of life appeared more leisurely further from the capital. Then St. Bees, being a compact seaside resort dominated by the School, allowed us to move about easily without cars, an important consideration with the heavy drinking sessions.

David Marshall's house, being next to the playing field and 'open all hours', became the control centre, the place to go if you'd forgotten where you were staying. And generally, because cricket tours were less numerous to that part of the country, we were welcomed with open arms by the locals, happy to be entertained by some, at least, of our antics.

My second tour gave me one of my treasured cricket memories. Of all the club grounds I've ever played on, or been to, my first sight of Eskdale made by far the greatest impact. Three of us pulled into the car park behind the Bower House pub, which also served as the Ground entrance, and strolled across to the gate to take a look at things.

I was stunned by the towering scale and proximity, of the steep hill immediately to the south. Like something out of a John Ford Western, I half expected a line of Indians on horseback to appear along the top. Surely the most spectacular backdrop to any cricket ground?

Then as I looked down to the Ground itself I was surprised, shocked even, to see sheep all over the place, including the square. They'd left ample droppings to mark their wanderings, and no real attempt had been made to keep them off the square.

There was only one chap on the Ground, and he was busy pushing a

The pre-match scene at Eskdale

small motor mower down the track. As I watched its progress, the handle could clearly be seen bouncing up and down, as it followed the undulating contours of the surface. The significance of this dawned on the three of us at the same time. We exchanged meaningful glances, including a fair portion of fright, and agreed we'd make it a very friendly match indeed, with only dead slow bowling allowed.

Next, we went round to the pavilion, not much bigger than a large, wooden, garden shed. The inside was like a miniature club cricket museum, with old brown bats with perished grips, split, pimply rubber gloves, and cricket balls unravelling, with string hanging down to the floor. For me, the whole set-up was absolutely delightful, and we later enjoyed a truly rustic, village cricket match, before adjourning to the Bower House.

After the sociable evening match at Eskdale on the Wednesday, the afternoon game at Gosforth on Thursday was a serious contest with some close finishes over the years. The strongest memory now is perhaps the magnificent teas, but two incidents on the field spring to mind. There was the day Nick Wright made 154, then the highest individual score in St. James's history. During the course of that epic, he peppered the main road with sixes, much to the annoyance of a gang of workmen who were trying to put down a new tarmac surface.

On another occasion something went wrong with the wicket preparation; our opener pushed forward to the first ball from the Gosforth quickie, and was covered all over with grass and soil as the pitch surface 'exploded'. Play was held up while he wiped his face and brushed down clothing, but what happened after that I can't remember.

We were also given a great welcome and much hospitality, including meat pies and mushy peas, in the evening after the Friday game against Cockermouth. This match had the considerable bonus of being played on a high quality square and outfield, developed for Minor County matches.

The routine we evolved was to meet at the 'Roundabout' pub just up the road, for bar billiards and lunch before the game. On our first visit B-P fashioned one of his classic one liners, as we piled into the bar and were waiting service. During a lull in the chat, B-P spotted three stuffed deer's heads on the wall above the bar, the type with no plaque, just the neck attached to the wall. With perfect timing he nodded towards them and quipped:

'Good God, they must've been travelling!'

In the all-day Saturday match against the School XI, we always put out our best team, and made a concerted effort to uphold our reputation as a strong club side. This we usually managed to do – I don't think we lost a game over the whole 17 years of the Tour – though we had to fight hard at times. And the boys of course, were razor keen to beat us or at least gain an honourable draw.

A memorable occasion in a School match one year, was when Peter

Beecheno was put on to bowl. Beech, then 54 years, had come on his only Tour, mainly for a break with the lads, and to sample the watering holes. Although suffering from a heavy cold and slightly hung-over, he was soon wheeling away with his customary nagging accuracy. When we finally prised him away from the crease, he'd got the remarkable figures of: 18 overs, 17 maidens, 4 wickets for 1 run. And, as he was quick to point out, the run came off a no-ball!

It was fascinating to watch the boys struggling to score runs. They'd been thoroughly coached in their defensive technique, and taught attacking strokes for the loose ball, but not been told what to do if every ball was on perfect line and length.

For the Sunday all-day match David Marshall used to scour around to get out the strongest side he could find, and it always a hard fought contest, honours about even overall. He had contacts with Whitehaven, who played in the North Lancashire League, and their professional would be enticed to front a side, made up with some good local club players.

When the Tour settled into it's regular format, the heart of affairs became the front Bar of the Queens Hotel. It was not much bigger than an ordinary domestic lounge, dimly lit, with a few small tables, and the bar across one end. It only took a dozen Tourists, plus a few regulars, to find everyone packed together, with fug, temperature and consumption rate rising rapidly.

There were over 20 tourists when the event reached peak popularity in the mid-'80's, some going mainly for golf, and booking all available rooms at the Hotel. With everyone jammed in the Bar, we effectively took over the place and, as residents, were able to drink beyond normal closing time.

The intimacy of those marathon sessions has left us all, in a sense alcohol brothers, if not blood brothers. Most of us were around my age, under much the same domestic pressures, and the Tour provided an annual opportunity to let our hair down. No subjects were off limits, as the jokes, repartee, and banter reached a crescendo, fuelled by drinks booked to the kitty. Usually we started on pints, but the hard men switched to Bloody Mary's later on.

Around mid-night, with most inhibitions shed, we'd launch into a

Morning 'refresher' in the back garden of the Queen's

sing-song. It would start with two or three in close harmony, genuinely trying to create a pleasant sound, accompanied by Charles Harrison on guitar. This would then steadily degenerate, as more and more joined in, with raucous, full throated renditions of any song that came to mind. This unholy row always finished with the Tour favourites, 'The Sloop John B' and 'Sweet Caroline', though hardly recognisable as such.

There were initially, protests from the other guests and neighbours, but they soon gave up, finding it easier to join in.

The rate of drink consumption certainly increased because we ran a kitty, and, in the heat of the moment, one could easily forget who was paying for it. For the earlier Tours the rate was set at £5 per day each, later increased by inflation to £10.

The kitty and all money matters were smoothly handled by Ian Heath, nicknamed 'the Godfather', and he organised supplementary whip rounds when necessary. Hardened as he became, even he was seen to raise an eyebrow when, after one outrageous thrash, he was presented with a bill for £200, at a time when beer was less than a pound a pint.

A fond memory from those evenings in the Queens, was of Tony Sweetman who, as time wore on, seemed to slide into a world of his own. His speech slowed and he rambled around trying to make his point, as listeners' attention wandered.

I can still see him now on his first Tour, glass tucked under elbow, eyes towards the ceiling, addressing the assembled throng, with almost religious fervour. His eventually completed sentence was something like:

'Good God, after two hours in this place, I can forget I've got a wife, kids, mortgage, grasping bank manager, unreasonable boss and impossible mother-in-law!'

It was an interesting observation the first time, well worth waiting for, but on subsequent Tours when he got round to the ritual repeat, we just left him to get on with it.

No-one managed to go on all 17 Tours up to '89, but I, and a dozen others, went on ten or more. It was great that we always had people with wit and personality to keep the fun going, and of course, having shared the experiences, we developed a fund of stories. It's these silly, humorous incidents we all remember now, when most else is forgotten. In any order, I've written up what I think are the most re-told, with due credit to those involved.

Jock Kydd had great difficulty getting away for his first Tour; it took weeks of delicate negotiations before his wife reluctantly gave permission. But there were strings; he would have to leave the Tour early Sunday, make his way to the house of his parents-in-law near Crewe, and pay them a lengthy social visit, including Sunday lunch.

On the Tour Saturday it was one boozy whirl of sessions at the School buffet and the Queens, but he managed to get up in time to catch the train on Sunday morning. Though distinctly groggy, he found his way to the house, looking quite presentable in suit, collar and tie.

Unscrambling his brain for the small talk, Jock even contrived an interest in his father-in-law's kitchen garden, but when lunch was served food was the last thing he wanted, despite his father-in-law's proud announcement that all vegetables were home grown.

Presented with a heaped plateful of roast and three veg, Jock took the first mouthful with a great sense of foreboding, knowing there was no chance of finishing the meal. The combination of Theakston's Old Peculiar and asparagus tips proved a potent cocktail, and with the second mouthful he threw up violently across the table, before slumping forward unconscious onto his plate.

It was a disappointing finish to a valiant effort, though Jock steadfastly claimed he'd carried out his side of the bargain. What his wife said on hearing the gruesome details, is not public knowledge.

The pavilion on the School playing fields was an ancient wooden affair, complete with heavily splintered floor and basic plumbing. We were given the only changing room and, as we played two games over the weekend, used to leave our kit there overnight.

Ian Boyd-Pain possessed a distinctive cricket bag, inherited from his father, of conventional style but covered in bright green cord carpet. When he left it overnight one year, someone thought it would be a good idea to nail it to the floor, and had come prepared with tools for the job. No sooner said than done, the kit was taken out, the hardboard bottom thoroughly nailed to the floor and the clothes replaced.

All eyes were on B-P as we packed to leave the next day, but things didn't quite work out as expected. He tried to lift the bag, then pulled hard again, only to end up with the top half in his hand. Realising he'd been set up, he simply scooped up the kit and left the rest there saying, "'bout time I had a new cricket bag!'

A bright blustery morning, and Pickering, Woodward, Harrison and Green decided on a trip to the beach, to blow away the cobwebs with a kickabout using a cheap plastic football. They enjoyed half an hour's lively exercise before Woodie, going for the big clearance, sliced the ball twenty yards out to sea.

With no-one prepared to get wet, and a strong breeze blowing it further out, the ball was abandoned and they strolled off round the bay. Suddenly there was a flurry of excitement, as the lads watched the St. Bees lifeboat being launched, all eyes swivelling across the horizon, searching for flares or a vessel in distress.

Disappointingly, the lifeboat just swung round towards the beach, scooped up the plastic ball and returned to shore. Surprised and somewhat embarrassed, the lads were later formally presented with the ball by the lifeboat crew, who explained they'd used the incident as a rapid response exercise.

Accommodation for Huntly Taylor and Mike Woodward was arranged one year, in a caravan parked in the yard of Tony Coates house, and it had no electricity, only Calor gas.

During the Saturday match Huntly damaged a finger, a hairline fracture was diagnosed and it had to be strapped to the next one with cotton wool, gauze and tape. Fortunately it didn't prevent a good session in the Queens and, with Woodie, he set off in pitch darkness for home in the early hours.

As they stumbled across the yard into the caravan, priority was to light a gas candle on the wall, a tricky operation at the best of times. Lighted match in one hand, Huntly fiddled to get it going, the only result being he set fire to his broken finger, the cotton wool proving highly flammable.

Huntly's first reaction was to bang the fingers on the table, resulting in an excruciating stab of pain. Next he tried to blow the fire out, only fanning the flames. Getting desperate, he turned to Woodie for assistance, to find him convulsed with laughter and incapable of doing anything. Finally he groped around to find a piece of cloth, and wrapped it round his fingers to smother the blaze.

When they eventually produced some light, Huntley was not best pleased to find the piece of cloth was his best shirt.

It was four o'clock when Tony Sweetman was weaving his way along the High Street, confident no-one else would be around that time in the morning. Suddenly a policeman on foot patrol appeared, a rare event in St. Bees, and strode purposefully towards him. As Tony was not entirely sober, he braced himself for the interview which went:

'Good morning sir!'

'Good morning constabule.'

'And where, might I ask, are you going sir?'

'To bed, hoccifer.'

'And where, might I ask, have you been sir?'

'Marshall's'

'And what's that sir, some kind of night club?'

Tony's brain was incapable of suitable response.

The deadpan wit of Ian-Boyd Pain took time to fathom, and Nigel Cook was a unwilling victim, running into it on his debut for the Club as well as his first Tour.

Nigel made his first appearance for St. James's in a Sunday game against Basingstoke and North Hants on the Mays Bounty Ground, very much a prestige fixture for us. The new boy arrived with substantial cricket bag, confidently introducing himself with a firm hand-shake all round. Tall, slim and smartly dressed, he had all the hall-marks of a top-drawer 'chap', and the whispered consensus was we'd gained a 'star'. (I wasn't entirely sure about that, as I felt his kit looked too new, or under-used.)

B-P, captain on the day had elected to bat, and everyone got changed as he drew up the order. Looking at the newcomer, B-P put on his most business-like voice and asked:

'Tell me Nigel, what do you do, cricket-wise?'

Always a loaded question, the reply should be modestly self-effacing while disclosing some relevant information. I thought Nigel pitched his answer perfectly with:

'Well, if I do anything Ian, I'm a slow-medium bowler.'

Quick as a flash, B-P's firm, even officious, response was:

'Great Nigel, would you open the batting then please?'

Nigel's face was a picture, as he stood stunned, eyes swivelling around, while he fought to believe what he'd just heard.

The travelling arrangements for Nigel's first Tour were suitably complex, as befitted a high powered businessman. He planned to drive to St. Bees, taking in appointments with clients on the way, but had been told it was essential he arrived for the six o'clock start at Eskdale, as only ten other players had promised to be there on time.

On the day, traffic caused Nigel to slip behind the clock, but by going flat out across the Lakes, he raced into the Eskdale ground at 6.15, with the match just under way. Screeching to a halt, he grabbed his kit and rushed into the pavilion, only to find B-P scoring and no other Tourist around. In fact two players had arrived unexpectedly, making 12 available, and when Nigel anxiously asked B-P what was happening, his straight-faced reply was:

'There's good news and bad news Nigel. The good news is you're not playing, the bad news is you're taking over as scorer in five minutes time.'

Nigel was not in the mood to see the funny side of that remark, picked up his kit, stormed back to his car, and left the ground at speed, not to be seen again for 24 hours.

Greg Mathews had come over from Australia for the '80 season as the Whitehaven professional, before going on to become a Test cricketer. David Marshall recruited Greg, his 'secret weapon', for the Sunday match against us that year. Going in at three, Greg scored a faultless 100 not out, before putting down nine overs, taking four for 33.

While his cricketing talent was obvious, he was also full of backchat and abrasive comment, clearly being at the height of his anti-Pom phase. No-one rose to the bait, and innuendo about parentage, intelligence and virility, was allowed to pass unchallenged. But he went too far at one point, when he implied we were unable to hold our beer, causing deep offence among the senior Tourists. It was agreed suitable action would have to be taken in the Queens that evening.

After the game, as soon as Greg arrived, Charles Harrison, Mike Woodward and others homed in on him, plying him with a mixture of drinks, while apparently downing their own as if there was no tomorrow. Skilfully, the person in front of him, forcing the pace, was rotated in shifts, but Greg fought on gamely, trying to match them glass for glass. After two hours of relentless pressure, Greg's eyes closed, he emitted a lengthy sigh, and slid unconscious to the floor.

With the Club's honour restored, he was carried outside to be loaded into a car for the journey home. But there was more indignity in store. The driver, on seeing the state of young Greg, said:

'This is my new car. I'm not having 'im in here in that state, put 'im in the boot!'

Qasim Omar, the Pakistan test player, was another recruit to David Marshall's XI one year, and scored an elegant fifty before giving his wicket away. But another year there was an amusing incident when two young Pakistanis were in the XI, neither appearing to speak English. In the field all afternoon, they nattered away incessantly in their native tongue, apparently having something to say about every ball. Our umpire, Barry Foreman, had spent some time in India during the War, and picked up a working knowledge of the local language. He'd listened to the two, and as they strolled off for tea, he broke into their conversation, in Urdu, with: 'Good afternoon gentlemen, I trust you enjoyed your session in the field.'

The two players were absolutely gobsmacked, stopping dead in their tracks unable to believe their ears. Barry then explained briefly about his Indian experiences, and touched other areas of common interest, before they reached the pavilion. Clearly well in the driving seat, he finished with the parting shot:

'Oh, and by the way gentlemen, there's nothing wrong with my mental health or my eyesight!'

Dick Packham was an enthusiastic Tourist, and responsible for some of the best humorous moments.

He and others were shopping in Workington High Street one day, when they came to a dress shop, and paused to watch a girl assistant trying to fix 'Sale' banners inside the main window. Holding the top corners of a sign about waist height against the glass, she twisted her head down to see if it was level.

Ever the gentleman, Packham stepped forward and started signalling, 'up a bit, down a bit', to help her get the level right. Glad of his assistance, when he mouthed to her that he'd hold the corners, gesticulating with his thumbs, she readily nodded in agreement.

Carefully, he then pressed firmly against the glass in the right places, giving her the nod that she could let go. She stood up as everyone outside, cheering, watched the banner float gracefully to the floor.

After a long session at David Marshall's house, by five in the morning everyone had left except Dick Packham, Phillip Parsons and Graham Smith. Too late to go to bed, a sobering cup of coffee seemed in order, but unable to find any milk the idea was abandoned. Then Packham, unwilling to admit defeat, jumped up and announced:

'Right, let's go and find a cow to milk.'

After the derisive laughter, the question as to whether he possessed the necessary skills was brushed aside, with words to the effect he'd forgotten more about milking than Dan Archer ever knew.

They set out for the nearest field with cows, but when they came face to face Packham got cold feet. Stealing milk from a cow probably being a serious offence, there was also a real chance of being caught by the farmer, so they settled for a sheep as second best.

With sheep all over the next field, the only problem was how one or two could be cornered and held. It was decided that Packham would rush about shepherding them through a gap in the hedge, while Parsons and Smith waited the other side to grab one each as they came through.

Packham did all the leg work, weaving around driving the sheep into the gap, and when he followed through last, he was confident he'd find two sheep firmly held. Instead he found Parsons and Smith standing there looking extremely – I'm sorry I can't think of another word – sheepish.

Surprised and a bit annoyed, Packham quizzed the two, but only got an embarrassed, mumbled apology. Apparently, as yuppies and city slickers, they'd no idea how to tackle the task, half expecting their quarry to have handles and warning labels on!

Dick Packham also stars in the most retold of all St. Bees stories and, bearing in mind the state of his brain at the time, it was undoubtedly a brilliant piece of repartee.

In the early hours, he and others were wending their way back to their various digs, with everywhere long since closed for the night. As they crossed the railway line, they noticed a light still on in the small French restaurant.

Suddenly and irrationally Packham said; 'I feel hungry', and started thumping on the front door of the restaurant, shouting repeatedly; 'Open up, open up!'.

The others thought he'd taken leave of his senses, but he persisted, pounding on the door again and again. Eventually the owner, absolutely furious at this disturbance, marched to the front door, flung it open and demanded:

'What the hell do you want?'

Packham's instant and now legendary reply was:

'Well, we'll start with the whitebait!'

One snag of the Tour was the long drive to St. Bees; it could take the best part of a day with stops en route. Then one year Bill Smith announced he was solving this problem, at a stroke, by chartering a light aircraft to take the strain. It seemed a great idea, and the rest of us started serious horse-trading, to try and get the spare seats.

All arrangements made, on the day Smith, with selected pals Dick Packham, John Cooper and Ian Boyd-Pain, were chauffeur driven to Shoreham Airport. They piled their luggage in a heap at the agreed assembly point, while they waited for the pilot. Each was carrying cricket kit, a golf bag, and a suitcase of personal clothing.

When the pilot arrived, he took one look at the mound of kit and, with weary expression, pulled out a pocket calculator. He then asked each in turn how much they weighed, totting up the answers before doing a few more calculations. Then he announced;

'Right, I can take a maximum of 10 kilos of luggage.'

Stunned, the four fliers had to scramble around, grabbing a few essential items to put in one case, to come within the limit. This done, the chauffeur was despatched post haste to Kings Cross station, to send the remaining luggage by parcel service to Carlisle.

The plane, a Piper Cessna, had a seat next to the pilot, two smaller ones behind, (effectively sitting on the drinks cabinet and the toilet), with the fourth perched behind them. Wedged in, the four enjoyed the two and a half hour flight without mishap, though the route involved various zigzags and detours over the sea, to avoid Heathrow, Luton and Manchester Airports.

Landing safely at Carlisle, they took a taxi for the 40 mile trip to St. Bees, stopping twice for lubrication. Having made their triumphal entry to the Queens, they'd only had time to retell the tale once, when another taxi arrived with the the rest of their luggage.

It made a good yarn, with plenty of scope for exaggeration and one-upmanship, and the four were well satisfied whatever the cost.

Emboldened by this success, the idea was floated the next year, of sailing to St. Bees in a 100 foot yacht, apparently available for the Tour period complete with five man professional crew. This caused a flurry of pipe dreams about a spectacular entrance to St. Bees bay, Club flag flying, reception party waiting ashore, and even perhaps a 21 gun salute.

Male bonding: Green and Pickering enjoy a convivial evening.

After the excited chat had died down, reality crept in; it's a shallow bay at St. Bees, and the yacht would have to moor some way off shore. The theory was that half a dozen inebriate tourists, would wend their way to the beach from the Queens, then row several hundred yards in a dinghy in the dark. It was impossible to contemplate this, without accepting one or more would be lost overboard per trip, seriously depleting the Tour party by the Sunday match.

But the plan was finally blown out of the water when it was learned the travelling time for the return journey, would be longer than time onshore at St. Bees!

The great wall building feat of the last Tour, crowned a series of events starting from the first, and ensured the Club left St. Bees in a blaze of glory.

On that Tour and subsequently, David Marshall arranged for two players to stay in the Headmaster's house, a situation fraught with potential disaster. Selection of suitable candidates involved anxious debate, as we needed people with a vague idea of the basic courtesies, and also capable of intelligible small talk, when heavily hung over at breakfast. Roger Green and Derek Pickering got the final nod, on the grounds they were blue chip 'chaps', effectively home from home, and also, marginally less likely to make improper suggestions to the Headmaster's wife.

Bearing in mind the Head had the power to throw us out, or perhaps not invite us the following year, the two turned on their silky charms the moment they stepped through the front door. Things went smoothly enough from day one, Green scoring bonus points by arriving for breakfast in a multi-coloured kaftan, adding class and diverting attention from his haggard appearance.

The one problem they had though, on returning from the Queens in the small hours, was negotiating the route to their first floor room. Whatever their state and however dark, the task had to be carried out as quietly as possible, to avoid waking the boys in the adjacent dormitory.

Over the years the two perfected a finely honed routine, Pickering reached for the light switch as Green went for the inner door handle, supporting each other as necessary. They then crept across to climb the baronial wooden staircase, a task involving great concentration, missing certain steps, treading on particular spots, to avoid creating the ear splitting squeaks and creaks that would otherwise result.

After dozens of successful entries, disaster struck on the '80 Tour when Pickering, more befuddled than usual, switched on the fire alarm by mistake. In the ensuing pandemonium, 60 boys were shepherded onto the lawn, believing it must be for real at four o'clock in the morning. Thankfully the Head, Malcolm Thynne, saw the funny side after all the abject apologies, but hinted of possible revenge.

With '89 the last Tour Malcolm had to act, so he devised a trap for the two on their early morning return on the Thursday. With conscript labour, he constructed a head high wall of tin cans, a few inches behind the inner door, and also intended to string up a trip wire, to simultaneously set off the burglar alarm and discharge a shot-gun at the top of the stairs. Wisely, he got cold feet about the last two items, reckoning the Governors would not be best pleased with these jolly japes, if the boys were rudely wakened the night before GCSE exams. When the two returned in the early hours, instinctively they were ready for trouble, so Green cautiously inched open the inner door. It just touched the bottom of the pile without knocking it over, and they then figured out a way of squeezing passed it. They went to bed and much enjoyed breakfast time, feigning ignorance of the cans during the small talk.

With the ball firmly in our court, a retaliatory wheeze had to be dreamt up quickly, to ensure we went out in a blaze of glory. All manner of crackpot schemes were bandied about, ranging from the totally impractical to the potentially lethal, until someone noticed that a new Sports Hall was being built near the Headmaster's house. David Knipe volunteered to carry out a discrete recce, reported back, and a viable plot was hatched.

After the Saturday session in the Queens, the Head and his wife left about midnight, having kept a wary eye on the Tour party all evening. When they'd had time to settle for the night, David Knipe passed a coded message to his hand picked squad, to rendezvous at 0200 hours on the School playing field. The motley crew assembled, some had blacked up – very effective as they were wearing cricket sweaters – and there was much giggling, shushing, and watering of shrubbery, until brought to a semblence of order.

Between hiccups, Knipe briefed his men on operational detail, the first stage being to move noiselessly and unseen to the Sports Hall site. Once there, they would ferry bricks to the Headmaster's house about a hundred yards away, to wall up the porch to his front door. The opening was some four feet wide by eight feet high, and the construction would have to be carried out silently, in near darkness.

The squad started off using the commando crawl to cross the playing field, but soon gave that up as too uncomfortable on top of a belly full of beer. Instead they yomped in single file at five yard intervals, with most of the noise generated by people shushing or telling others to keep quiet.

As they neared the site, Knipe wisely detailed Parsons to be the brick loader, as he was giggling most, and best kept furthest from the House. The main squad then ferried the bricks to feed the construction team, a task which required strength, stamina, stealth, and an ability to see in the dark. Also, it developed into a test of virility, those carrying six or eight bricks at a time passing caustic

The wall in place, the morning after.

comment on those carrying only four. (Total bricks moved were about 250, weighing half a ton.)

Knipe took personal command of the architecture in the porch, drawing heavily on his professional skills. He started the wall, using a nine inch thick stretcher and header construction, but having reached half height, decided to switch to four and a half inch single thickness. He had shrewdly assessed his team was wilting from the effort, enhanced by natural tiredness and the evening session.

As he neared the top he passed the signal down the line to stop supply, and for a few seconds the whole squad assembled in front of the porch, to silently marvel at the fruits of their labours.

The operation had taken forty five minutes of tough disciplined action and our heroes melted away to their beds well satisfied. There was just one unexpected hitch; Old Tom, a regular from the Queens, was encountered weaving his way across the playing fields, determined to take a look at the wall he'd heard so many whispers about. With operational secrecy in jeopardy, Knipe revealed his ruthless streak by ordering that he, 'be disposed of'.

The Head's family were in a rush to get away on holiday the next morning, Malcolm Thynne being the first to try and hurry through the front doors. I would love to know what the cultured, erudite Headmaster of a top public school says in such a situation. Presumably he wouldn't stoop to the 'f' word, but; 'golly gosh!', 'gadzooks!', or Puttie's old favourite, 'bother me!', all seem somewhat tame.

The 'Roll of Honour' for this magnificent episode, commanded by David Knipe, was: Roger Green, Charles Harrison, Bruce Nunn, Dick Packham, Philip Parsons, Derek Pickering, Peter Walton and Mike Woodward.

It was a fitting climax to the 17th and last Tour, a story much retold and exaggerated since, that ensured we departed the area with heads held high.

Bill Gunn and the author wind-up the last tour.

CHAPTER II

OUR LONG-SUFFERING WOMEN

My cricket life started pre-feminism, and it's difficult to believe now some of the things women put up with in the 'bad' old days. The men would decide what games they would play the next weekend, based on the Club requirements, strength of opposition and match venue. From then on, wives and girlfriends had to fit in, or be fitted in, around that timetable.

If women did attend the game, voluntarily or otherwise, they tended to be regarded at best as an unavoidable encumbrance, at worst as a distraction to the team's performance. Even at the after-match drinks session, they would be left to chat amongst themselves while the men discussed weightier matters, such as whether their umpire was bent or incompetent.

By recognising this injustice (with hindsight) from the outset, I hope St. James's womenfolk of my generation will be able to look back with a smile, and not too much repressed bitterness.

Though women were never allowed to umpire, scoring was a job they could be given with a dual advantage. It was not critically important if they made a mess of it, and it gave them something to do. Nevertheless, I treasure memories of two incidents when things didn't go to plan.

The first was a St. James's match in Preston Park, against St. Mathias on the Terrace pitch opposite the Pavilion. One of our players had arrived at the last minute, dressed in dinner jacket from the night before, with a young lady, Veronica, in tow. She looked dishevelled and slightly hung over, still wearing a full length, figure hugging, silver lamé dress with all the trimmings. It turned out she'd never seen a cricket match before, but, being a bubbling 'hooray Henrietta' type, was keen to get involved in the action.

Her opportunity arose immediately, as we were in the field and there was no-one to do the scoring. With shrieks of, 'what do I do, what do I do?', Veronica was handed the book, gazing in wonderment at the complexity of numbers, lines and squares. Gamely she struggled to grasp the basics, with much help from the other scorer; but knowing none of the names of our players didn't help.

The opposition scorer, who managed to keep two books going at once, while delivering a potted course on the fundamentals of the game, performed heroically. But inevitably there were problems, and after a few overs the umpires got irritated that, from the start, not one of their signals had been acknowledged. They held up play, walked to the boundary, and duly remonstrated with the offending ladies.

Having grasped the point Veronica took the positive view, grabbing her chance at interactive involvement in the game. From then on she more or less forgot about the nitty-gritty of scoring, but leapt up excitedly, waving her arms about, at any signal from the umpires.

We had a regular fixture at Rudgwick, near Horsham, and they had a small wheeled wooden scorebox, parked some distance from the main pavilion. It was about five foot square and eight foot high, with the numbers on the top of the front face. There was a desk across, two stools, large openable sliding windows, and an entrance door at the back. The whole thing was rickety and top heavy, but everything functioned and it served the purpose.

We were batting after tea on a cold, blustery day, and I'd been cajoled into scoring, from the start of our innings anyway. The opposition scorer was a woman a few years older than me, recently married to one of the Rudgwick players, and dressed for a theoretical, warm summer's day.

She soon made it clear in one way or another, she didn't like scoring, was cold and miserable, and certainly wasn't going to make small talk with the likes of me. Conversation was strictly limited to the niceties of scoring, 'three off the over?', 'he must have got an edge?', 'do you make it five byes?', 'which batsman was that?', and so on.

After half an hour the traumatic incident occurred when Derek Pickering had got into his stride, and lofted a powerful, high off-drive towards the scorebox. With tension rising rapidly, she put on a brave front, stating with studied calm:

'That looks as if it might be coming our way?'

Trying desperately to match her cool, I replied:

'Yes indeed; it does look as if it…'

We both realised at the same instant, the ball was coming through the glass front. She shrieked and we both ducked under the bench, clashing heads on the way, as the only place offering some shelter. The ball crashed through the glass, showering splinters around, richoteting about till it dropped to the floor. Stunned, we both stood up to look at each other, she being too shocked and distressed to speak.

I remember she used hair lacquer, all the rage at that time, and, with the sparkling shards of glass on the outside, looked like the Christmas fairy doll. Any laughter from me would not have been appreciated, to put it mildly, so I concentrated on removing the larger pieces, while showing great concern for her welfare.

But I was also presented with a dilemma; would she consider it intrusive of her person, if I gingerly removed a shard nestling on her bust along the top edge of her dress?

As I struggled with my conscience, thankfully the problem disappeared, when the door burst open and her husband and others arrived to rescue us. She collapsed into his arms in tears, before they left together, leaving me to sort myself out, and keep the show on the road.

When I started playing at club level, I automatically looked for a game every Saturday and Sunday; as a batsman both days were considered essential to keep in some sort of form. The possibilities of conflict with the opposite sex, were brought to my attention by a young 'star', who played for St. James's briefly, and appeared at each match with his attractive young lady, Melanie.

From the outset, she made a point of demonstrating her boredom and dislike for cricket, by refusing to look at the play, reading a book or feigning great interest in anything off the field. When her boyfriend was available, they would set off to stroll round the boundary, joyfully entwined. By the time they were half way round, they'd be a yard apart, and engaged in a fullscale slanging match.

This went on for a month or so, till one weekend he arrived for both games without her. To our polite enquiry as to Melanie's whereabouts, the reply was swift:

'It's all finished,... she didn't want me to play both games a weekend.'

Then he added the wistful afterthought:

'It's all a matter of priorities...'

My own 'courtship' went more smoothly a far as cricket was concerned, despite some gloriously chauvinistic behaviour. I met Carol at a Rugger Club dance in the winter, so there was no reason to broach the subject of cricket for some months. When I did, it was worrying to learn she'd never seen a game in her life, and the possibilty of conflict crossed my mind.

Things got off to an inauspicious start, when she made her own way by train to see her first match, the season's opener at Keymer and Hassocks at the end of April. Apart from the fact it'd been rained off, it didn't help that we'd rushed down the pub for a swift one before closing time; so she arrived at an empty ground.

But after the settling down period, Carol never accepted the role of grass widow, always happy to come along for the social side, do a bit of scoring if the Club was hard pressed, plus of course, teas.

In the '67 summer we decided to get married the following spring – best time for tax purposes I understood. During a session in the 'Cricketers' on Broadwater Green in late September, I mentioned we'd firmed up on an April wedding.

As a 'wind-up', the lads called an instant Committee meeting to consider the cricketing implications of this date. Held in a corner of the saloon bar it was decided, by a majority, that the date would have to be brought forward to avoid any conflict with pre-season nets. When I put this to Carol, telegraphing heavily it was just a joke, she saw no problem, so the big day was fixed for early January.

The next incident of note was when our daughter Lisa was born in the middle of a season. In those days, first time mothers had to stay in hospital for a fortnight, so a lot of visiting had to be done, especially at weekends. Carol was at Brighton General, and there were two Saturday visiting sessions, strictly between two-thirty and four, and seven and eight.

At that time I was Team Secretary, struggling to get sides out each week, and knew it essential to play myself. I explained the position at great length to Carol, seriously bored and fed up, and after a lot of smarm won permission to play, with the strict proviso I turned up on the dot for the evening visiting hour.

We fielded first in the match, at Stanmer Park, just a few miles from the Hospital. Everything was fine up to the tea interval, the opposition setting us a target of around 180. It was after this that sod's law took over with a vengeance. I had a word with the skipper, explaining that I had to leave the ground by six-forty come what may, and he was happy to put me up to number three.

The first snag was that the openers built up a steady 50 partnership, not being separated till twenty past six. As I walked out to bat, I decided my policy would be to play myself in for one over, then give it a whirl, on the probability I'd not last a second.

The plan worked initially, but when I launched into my strokes, textbook and crude, for once it all seemed incredibly easy. Thrashing the ball all round the park, I was unable to avoid the middle of the bat and enjoyed myself like never before.

Pausing for breath with my score nearing 40, I checked the time with the umpire and was horrified to learn it was quarter to seven. Instant suicide was essential so, I walked down the pitch, made sure I kept body and bat well away from the ball, and turned to watch it hit the stumps. (I was glad it hit the wicket, the 'keeper would probably have fluffed the stumping!)

Racing off the field with brief wave to acknowledge applause, I changed and got to the Hospital as fast as I could. But in spite of my best endeavours, it was still nearly twenty-five past seven before I hurtled through the Ward doors. To say I got a warm reception is an understatement, and the only lame excuse I could come up with was the church clock wasn't working.

Shamefully, we males plumbed the depths of chauvinism during the early '70's, when our offspring were mere babes in arms. Obviously our cricketing activities couldn't be disturbed, so wives would attend matches with prams, carry-cots, nappies, food, and the rest; to keep the babes warm and fed from the start till late in the evening.

After home matches, we used to drink in the County Oak pub in Patcham, which had a car park but no gardens or place to sit outside. Because children under age were not allowed inside, our wives were forced to sit in the cars outside, looking after the kids in carry-cots on the back seat. It was O.K. for an hour or so, but as evening wore on it became cold and dark, as well as being boring and miserable.

As a sop, and to demonstrate we weren't entirely uncaring, we would fetch them drinks occasionally, even perhaps, with the odd packet of crisps. To save us going outside (and getting cold) we would pass these out through the Men's Toilet window, holding them out in the dark until someone grabbed them.

I venture to suggest, thankfully, such despicable behaviour could never take place in today's world.

By the end of the '70's, a group of us thought it would be a 'good idea' to arrange a ladies match in Stanmer Park. We had a spare Sunday, which turned out to be a glorious day, so we arranged a picnic lunch with plenty of refreshments, before a scratch afternoon game.

For rules, we made it twenty overs a side, and the men had to bat and bowl wrong-handed. It surprised us how little our women actually knew about cricket, but things got under way after much explanation. We soon drew quite a crowd, intrigued by the frequent peels of laughter, some of whom were keen to join in, or send their kids out to play.

It was great fun, but as a contest it was hopelessly one-sided, none of the women having played any sport before. We decided the following year to increase the men's handicap; we had to bat wrong-handed, and bowl underarm and wrong-handed.

Still the men won easily, so next time we had the same plus the women's runs counting double and their innings lasting twice as long as ours. That went too far the other way, we had to score 185 off 10 overs, with the ball being rolled slowly along the ground!

Then we switched to stoolball, on the basis that men and women do play together in matches. But again – and I've played competitive stoolball – it's a skilful game, especially trying to bat without a backlift, so the men dominated once more. Then we gave up.

For years, decades even, I was totally ignorant of the process of producing sandwiches, cakes, and cups of tea, for a club cricket match, this area of expertise being classified strictly female. I never queried the mechanics of the operation, only aware I paid part of my

Frantic action in the '81 Ladies match at Stanmer Park

match fee in order to consume same. Most of my efforts were always concentrated on getting the biggest plateful, or best selection of cakes.

One of the strongest literary images in club cricket, or more correctly village cricket, is that of the genteel tea lady, happily whipping up cream scones in the pavilion kitchen. Invariably it's also a beautiful, cloudless day, the game is being played in the friendliest, sporting spirit, and class barriers are crumbling as the vicar explains the art of leg spin to the blacksmith.

I can think of no better way to shatter that cosy image, than detailing the harsh realities of preparing teas for a match in Stanmer Park.

The more I think about it now, I feel quite guilty; I didn't realise the unhygienic and squalid conditions we'd expected our womenfolk to work in.

Everything had to be produced from a dirty, lean-to hut, about six foot square, in front of the stable block used for the changing rooms. Inside was an ancient, chipped, porcelain sink, with cold tap only, and a rotting, wooden draining board. Otherwise, there was just a rickety trestle table and a couple of benches on the rough brick floor.

There was one window on the front, which opened like a pair of doors, and this, and the main door, were closed up and the hut unused during the week. It was overhung by a tree and close to bushes, making it semi-dark inside on all but the brightest days, and the odour and ambience were not enhanced by its proximity to the mens outside toilet.

The hut having been surrendered to nature for a week, when the tea-lady arrived to prepare for a game, she would be greeted with a dank, musty smell, cobwebs draped across corners, spiders running about the floor, and silverfish darting around the draining board. First task would be to work with cloth and brush, trying to clean things up a bit, and scare away the larger insects.

With no hot water available, next priority was to get the Burco boiler on; the Club had purchased a second-hand one, stored during the week in someone's garage (and frequently forgotten on the day).

Having sorted the basics out, she could then get on with the sandwiches and cakes, trying to keep door and windows shut till it became too hot. This was because, in late summer particularly, as soon as there was a smell of jam or cream, the flies and wasps from the surrounding greenery would move in, eventually taking the place over.

It must be said, from these primitive conditions some fine teas were produced, and few complaints voiced. Players would collect their rations from the hut and sprawl around on the pocket lawn nearby, or, if feeling reckless, try sitting on one of the ancient, wooden benches.

In an incident now enshrined in Club folklore, Deedee Pickering, in the first flush of enthusiasm as a cricket wife, decided to break the mould of the established tea menu. For her stint one day, and the expected delectation of all, she scrapped conventional sandwiches, and replaced them with a single, open, vindaloo curry sandwich per person. In the days when Indian restaurants and take-aways were new to this country, the idea was refreshingly bold and innovative.

Unfortunately, the pile of brown stuff on a slice of white bread looked somewhat unappetising, and more to the point, no-one knew what to do with it. There was no cutlery, and it was too runny to pick up with bare hands so, sadly, every portion was returned untouched.

I've always thought though; it was a tea ahead of its time.

Over the years the format for a standard club cricket tea has changed little: two or three halves of sandwiches, a scone, two cakes or pieces of cake, plus a cup of tea. But the variety and quantity is still, thankfully, variable even in the supermarket age.

I remember our first away fixture at an 'up market' Surrey club, with a lovely ground, pavilion and pub. There seemed to be a lot of activity in the kitchen all afternoon, so we were disappointed when tea was finally revealed. It consisted of a single scone – no doubt home-made – with fresh cream, washed down with a plastic cup of orange squash. If that wasn't bad enough, we were then charged one pound fifty, when the going rate was a pound.

For my generation of St. James's players, asked which was the finest tea they'd ever experienced, the answer would always be Firle. One of the oldest Clubs in the country, with lovely ground in Firle Park, it was a great setting for a game, the only problem being the small wooden pavilion without main services. Because of this, for our Sunday 'friendly' fixtures, tea was taken upstairs in the 'Ram' pub just outside the ground entrance.

The room was set out with proper, mahogany dining tables and chairs, with spotless, white linen and place settings. Down the centre of each table would be bowls of salad stuff, cold meat and cheeses. In addition plates of creamed scones, buttered bread and cakes, and, I particularly recall, individual glass bowls full of home-made jams such as plum, gooseberry and greengage.

It seems the teas were prepared as a labour of love, by two or three ladies, I would think players mums, determined to provide the ultimate in quality and quantity. They had no time for chit-chat, concentrating on the task in hand, pouncing to freshen a half empty tea cup, or plate of goodies. It should also be added, the teas were limitless, one could sit and eat for as long as one wanted, the good ladies would re-stock the table continuously.

As its reputation grew, the Firle teas started to pose problems for the Team Secretary. Having struggled for weeks with only eight available, he would find various Vice-Presidents, retired or fringe players, come out of the woodwork with; 'haven't had a run out this season old boy, how about Firle on Sunday?' Suddenly he'd be earnestly selecting from sixteen.

I developed my own tactics for Firle matches where I felt, uniquely, it was much preferable to field first. Then as we walked off for tea, I would clamp my arm round the skipper's shoulders and say something like:

'I've had a fair run up the order this season skip, I don't mind going down to six or seven this week.'

Apart from scoring brownie points, this would ensure I could extend my tea beyond the normal interval. Without rush, I could sit and gorge myself in an unseemly manner, and allow time for a couple of circuits of the ground to walk off the bloated feeling.

It was about this period I remember a superb incident of social class, as applied to a cricket tea. We had a chap called David Jameson join the Club briefly, until in fact, we rumbled he was a useless cricketer. I don't know too much about his background, but he'd been to a top public school and certainly had oodles of money.

He turned up for an away match one day, in his black Bentley saloon, with his good lady elegantly at his side. We fielded first, while she read a book sitting in the passenger seat, not venturing out to mix with the lower orders. But it was in the changing room at the start of the tea interval, that David brought attention to himself by an unusual comment:

'Skipper, I shall not be taking tea today, thank you.'

I watched him closely from then on. He washed, carefully combed his hair, changed into brown brogues, neckerchief and multi-coloured blazer, then left the room. Some minutes later, I glanced out the window and was stunned to see how tea is taken in real style.

Mrs Jameson had set up a small circular table, with lace edged white table cloth, parasol, and two wooden slatted chairs. The table was prepared with all silver, teapot, jugs, bowls, cups, saucers and plates, some laden with sandwiches, scones and cakes.

The good lady was wearing a long blue floral dress, white gloves and shoes, and a straw picture hat with matching ribbon. I couldn't believe it was intended, but the blue of her dress perfectly matched the parasol. They sat down opposite each other and she proceeded to pour him a cup of tea, having satisfied herself he was ready and it was properly brewed.

It made a charming picture, amusingly out of place in surroundings which I think were a public park, emphasized by the odd scrawl of graffiti on the pavilion walls.

From those gentler days, tea-making has become more of a chore with an element of feminine reluctance creeping in. One of the old school, Derek Pickering, was skipper of a Sunday match at Hartfield in the mid-'80's, when after a sumptuous tea he felt obliged to express his feelings to the senior tea-lady.

She was cleaning a formica top as Derek, in front, started his speech: 'May I take this early opportunity, of expressing my sincere thanks, on behalf of my Club and myself, for what, in my humble opinion, but with more than thirty years experience in club cricket, is undoubtedly...'

The lady refused to look up, but the dish-cloth circled noticably faster as he droned on.

'...one of the finest teas it has ever been my good fortune to consume...'

When she was sure he'd finished, she looked up and with false smile said:

'Creep!!'

A lot changed from the balmy days of Firle in the '60's to the hard-nosed, liberated days of Bolney in the late '80's. It was a First team League fixture and, unwittingly, our players had arrived at the end of a major dust-up within the home club. I don't know the exact details of the row, but I've pieced the gossip together and, with a splash of 'artistic licence', I believe this is roughly what happened.

It seems some of the Bolney players had arrived early, to open up the ground and do the pre-match chores. They had with them two young ladies, say Sharon and Tracey, both already disillusioned with the unwanted roles of grass widow and tea-maker.

Their boyfriends, aware of the girls' feelings, tried to put a cheery gloss on things, and helpfully offered to sort out details when it came round to teas. Nothing had been organised, so the idea was the two girls would go down to the village store, buy the necessary, then prepare the teas in time for the interval.

A shopping list was drawn up and the trip about to start when, fatally, one of the men threw in a casual afterthought:

'Oh by the way Sharon; perhaps we could try one or two different sandwich fillings this week?'

Sharon ignited; she told the stunned men exactly what she thought about cricket, tea-making, the role of women in a male dominated society, and everything else including the weather. She ended her tirade by telling her man, in some anatomical detail, precisely where he could stick his sandwiches.

With that the two ladies flounced out of the pavilion, not to be seen again. When two of our rather more mature ladies arrived about four o'clock, they were (unhurriedly) appraised of the situation. As old hands they agreed to go down to the store and sort out the best they could. There was nothing much left by the time they got there, so tea for all was a packet of crisps and cup of orange squash.

Now the sexes are more equal, cricket teas are becoming a joint effort with nothing taken for granted. Players sometimes arrive at the ground with their kit in one hand and a cardboard box of sandwiches under the other arm. Or they have to sprint off the field at four-thirty to switch on the urn.

With all this in mind, I must pay tribute to my wife Carol for all the hundreds of teas she's organised, often in grotty conditions, without complaint (or involving me!). Carol is often asked to throw together a quick poem, for a party or special occasion of some sort. It's an acquired taste, but here's one she's written to celebrate her tea-making activities over the years:

DOING IT FOR 26

At the beginning of April the anticipation
is almost like getting a fix,
through those long winter days
I've been working out ways,
how to please the whole 26.

The question as always is whether they think
I'll be ready, able and willing,
when they're all on a bender
I hope they'll remember
who's sarnies had the best fillings.

Gone are the days in that Stanmer Park shed
it was worse than a dirty old cellar,
as I buttered my bread
there was always the dread
of an outbreak of salmonella.

When they'd had a tough game I always tried hard
to please all those strapping big men,
and I hope they'd agree
when I'd poured out the tea
I'd never shout - 'How was that then!'

As I filled my tea urn my thoughts really ran wild
because just for a very short time,
whether they want me or not
I'm all that they've got
the umpires – the teams – were all mine.

At the end of September I feel so deflated
as I return to the Crowborough sticks,
but it's been a great season
and I smile with good reason
'cos I've been 'doing it' for 26.

The tea shed at Stanmer Park, now in advanced decay

CHAPTER 12

SOME FAVOURITE STORIES

There's nothing much new in the game of cricket, but if you're present when the unusual occurs, there may be a special slant that makes it more amusing, or memorable.

An example that comes to mind is of the ball getting 'plugged', after a shot lofted into the outfield. I saw this happen at Brook House near Lindfield, in an end of season match, after a horse had left hoofmarks in the soggy turf during the week.

The twist in this case was that the nearest fielder, raced round for the catch, couldn't quite make it, and lunged his foot despairingly forward to intercept the ball. It 'plugged' into the mark a split second before the fielder's boot scraped over it, pushing the ball right down almost burying it.

Rushing back to the spot, the fielder dropped to hands and knees, frantically trying to dig the ball out. He hadn't seen the funny side, glancing frequently towards the wicket, worried the batsmen would sneak too many extra runs. In fact they had to be satisfied with three, the umpires deciding, on some basis, that enough was enough.

I'm a strong believer in the theory that, the more disorganised any activity is, the greater potential for naturally occurring humour. Grassroots club cricket, usually being much less regulated and organised than the first class game, is a case in point. There must be thousands of good stories sculling around out there, so in this chapter I've written up some that particularly appealed to me, gleaned from colleagues or witnessed myself.

——❧——

Frank Osborne has a charming anecdote from the '50's, when teams usually travelled to matches by bus. Frank was playing for Middle Street Old Boys, a Brighton side, for a game at Chailey, a village about five miles north of Lewes.

The team assembled and boarded the bus at the Pool Valley depot, filling up the luggage space under the stairs with eleven sets of kit plus the Club bag. Their route to Chailey took them through Lewes, with a stop at the main depot, where another cricket team clambered on board.

To the conductor's irritation, kit overflowed onto the front seats, and there was quite a kerfuffle before everyone settled down. The two sides got chatting, and of course, someone asked a Lewes player:

'Who're you playing against?'

When he replied, 'Chailey', there was a pregnant pause in the conversation.

They decided to carry on, and when they met the Chailey side, the mix-up was pinned on the home Fixture Secretary. It was amicably agreed that Middle Street should play the Lewes side, and a match got under way.

All was sweetness and light till the Chailey President arrived. He was outraged that Chailey weren't playing on their own ground, so a coin was tossed to decide who the opposition should be. Middle Street lost, got changed, and caught the next bus home.

My pal Puttie got married later in life than usual, so his so-called friends were determined to organise a stag night he'd never forget. On the day, getting him legless turned out to be a push over, and he was last heard apologising for his slurred speech, before crashing out. Derek Pickering and John Moore then drove him back from the Brighton pub to his flat in Rottingdean, making sure he was safely indoors. By then around one o'clock, when the two left Rottingdean on the coast route, they were immediately waved to a halt at a road block – apparently there'd been a major burglary in the village shortly before. A policeman peered in the window with torch and asked Derek, the driver:

'Would you mind telling me what's in the boot, sir?'

To which Derek replied:

'Balls!'

Barely able to contain his anger the P.C. ordered:

'Right; out of the car and open up the boot.'

Derek calmly did so to reveal three small cardboard boxes, each containing a dozen new cricket balls.

Bill Bailey has done a great deal of sterling work for St. James's over the years, particularly on the maintenance of the Ditchling Ground. A down to earth, no nonsense type, he was the architect of two amusing and unusual incidents.

We were fielding in mid-afternoon in a Sunday match at Stanmer Park, on a fine sunny day in the late '70's. There were lots of tourists milling around and also, I believe, a Christening at the Church with more people wandering about in their Sunday best.

A batsman hooked a ball for six, which landed smack in the middle of the pond, bobbing about on the surface. With nothing better to do, a crowd soon gathered to see what would happen next. In fact the first move was to fetch a ten foot bamboo pole, with net tied to the end, kept in the groundsman's store for this purpose.

But tantalisingly, a fielder at full stretch, with two others clinging on to stop him falling in, was still a foot or two short; the ball by then stationary in a scum of green pollen.

With the crowd still growing, Bailey grew tired of the pussyfooting around and decided to sort the matter out. He stripped off down to his jockstrap, grabbed the net, and plunged into the murky water. He soon scooped up the ball, climbing out to enthusiastic applause all round.

When I was Fixture Secretary, before we had our own ground, I was always on the lookout for good new Sunday away games. After some years of trying, I was pleased to arrange a game against Glynde, at their splendid ground in the village. Everything went smoothly for a few seasons, until Bill Bailey all but lost us the fixture for good.

We were batting first on a wet pitch, and Glynde had a quickish bowler who was getting the ball to lift awkwardly, soon putting our first three back in the pavilion. Bailey went in and found things just as difficult, getting hit on gloves or body every over. Glynde sensed they were on to a good thing, especially their over-enthusiastic silly mid-on, who crept in closer each ball.

The fateful delivery hit Bailey on his unprotected, front thigh, and looped gently up in the air in front of him. Immediately silly mid-on, no more than two yards away, started to tip forward to retrieve the ball. But as it fell Bailey took a huge swing at it, connected perfectly, and sent it first bounce through mid-wicket into the stream.

Silly mid-on reeled backwards in shock, realising the ball must have streaked inches passed the side of his head. The other Glynde players were, rightly, incandescent with rage, and play was held up while our side tried frantically to calm things down.

Remarkably, having played club cricket for at least ten years, Bailey didn't know a batsman can't take two hits at one delivery, so initially didn't understand the fuss. The atmosphere remained icy for the rest of the game, and when the Glynde President heard the story afterwards, he was so incensed he talked about phoning Lord's. Eventually things were smoothed over and Glynde saw the funny side of it, though I could easily have witnessed my first cricket fatality.

———⋙✦⋘———

Though it took place more than twenty years ago, I still wonder whether this episode was a 'wind-up'.

We were playing at Crowhurst Park, a postage stamp of a ground near Battle, which had the pavilion at a right angle to the pitch. I was fielding at square-leg when a wicket fell, and the batsman trudged past on his way to the boundary. As he reached the line, I swung round to take a look at the incoming player, and did a double take; the new batsman was wearing sun glasses, something I'd never seen before. What's more, the glasses were not the fancy, modern Polaroid or polychromic type, but old fashioned pieces of curved plastic painted black on one side.

I watched in amazement as he made his way to the wicket, all other indications being that he was something of a 'star' performer. When he got to the crease he was an age taking guard, cutting lines and V-shapes, digging trenches, until satisfied.

At this point, I thought he'd remember his sun glasses and remove same, but he didn't. The first ball came down, he pushed forward with a good looking defensive stroke, but fractionally late and was bowled. As he came towards me, he seemed genuinely peeved at getting out, beating the bat on the ground and mouthing a variety of oaths. When he reached me, I felt unable to offer the usual sympathetic, 'bad luck batsman!', so I said nothing. But he looked straight at me, cheeks flushed with anger, and said: 'Honestly, I just didn't see it'.

I had to choke back laughter, as he was deadly serious, and continued to the boundary cussing all the way.

I intended to tackle him about it after the game, but he went early and I didn't see him again.

———————

I captained St. James's occasionally when they were short (or desperate), and was due to do so for an all-day match at Godalming one year. It's a long journey for me and I got thoroughly lost, with no chance of making the 11.30 start. In fact only one car arrived in time, containing Huntly Taylor, Mark Whitlock, Charles Harrison and Ian Boyd-Pain.

The Godalming skipper seemed keen to get on with it, so Huntly assumed the captaincy and went out to do the honours. On the way to the wicket, he dropped heavy hints about traffic problems and being a bit short, hoping he'd be put in if he lost the toss. But the Godalming skipper showed no sympathy, and elected to bat immediately having made the correct call.

Our four took the field with B-P behind the stumps, and after careful deliberation, Huntly opted for a one one field, with Charles Harrison at cover and Mark Whitlock at mid-wicket. Unbelievably, Huntly bowled the first ball and the batsman spooned a dolly catch to Whitlock, who dropped it.

Remarkably, with accurate bowling both ends, Godalming didn't capitalise on the wide open spaces, and when the second car arrived after twenty minutes things returned to normal. In the end it was a close fought contest, and both sides compared notes in the bar afterwards.

Apparently there were only 11 people on the Ground at the start; we had four and they had seven, with no umpires or scorers. Their seven had been employed by two batting, two umpiring, two scoring, and one man padded up!

⇒◦◦◦⇐

Huntly Taylor got involved in a knock-out competition for the Association of Dispensing Opticians one year, and was asked to organise and skipper the local side. All teams were supposed to be drawn from the optical profession, and there were a few genuine players, but mostly the sides were non-cricketers, happy to have an afternoon off.

The team had to play the London area at Wood Green, and Huntly took Charles Harrison – a ringer – along to boost the bowling if needed. They drove to the location not knowing what to expect; it fact it was a public recreation ground. It was also one of those with public foot paths, with attendant rights of way, criss-crossing the outfield.

But when they strolled out to take a look at the wicket, they got a real shock. The park-keeper, keen to protect his square for a low grade match, had cut a pitch just off the main table. Right in the line between wickets and about two yards off halfway, was the cast iron inspection cover for the watering system.

The Sussex side batted first, scoring rapidly against weak opposition, and declared well past 200. As they took the field after tea, Huntly gathered his men round the offending inspection cover for a pep talk. He said in effect: 'we're all sensible people, it's only a joke game, there's no point in anyone getting hurt, so keep the ball well up all the time.

All went to plan until two tailenders got together, cutting and carving the ball around, and putting their team in with an outside chance of winning. Charles Harrison, who'd been tossing up gentle half volleys off three yards, was given the nod by Huntly to use his full run-up. He paced that out with some enthusiasm, and hurried in to bowl his first 'proper' ball.

In the heat of the moment, he put it down too quick and short, ricochetting off the inspection cover and felling the batsman with a sickening blow on the cheek. Fortunately he was not seriously hurt, but what Huntly vividly recalls was; 'the metallic click, followed by the skeletal clunk!'

⸻ ◈◈◈ ⸻

The St. James's match against Rottingdean in August '57 was, and remains, probably the most exciting the Club has been involved in since the Second World War. It was a home fixture in Stanmer Park, and there'd been heavy rain in the week drying rapidly on the Saturday.

We'd put together a strong side for this derby fixture, except for being one short. The pubs were scoured, and David Lewis, in his late forties and almost retired from the game, dragged out and pressed into action.

Rottingdean batted first and it soon became apparent the wicket was lethal; the ball either skidded through low, or cut the top and reared up alarmingly. Our main bowler was Sandy Farrar, a top class performer at any club level. With his high rocking action he could hit the deck hard, generating lift and bounce on most wickets. Bowling unchanged at Stanmer that day he was unplayable, survival for the batsman being a lottery. After an hour and a half of hopeful pushing and prodding, Rottingdean were all out for 17.

In the changing room between innings, the St. James's team realised the pitch was dreadful, but couldn't believe they could fail to score 18, even if they shut their eyes and swung at each ball. There was talk of reversing the batting order, but the skipper urged caution and said the first five could swap with the second five, leaving David Lewis at eleven.

The innings got under way, with Rottingdean determined to give as good as they got. They quickly scythed through the five tailenders, starting the real fight when the regular batsmen came in. Our men mounting a determined rearguard action, picked up a few singles in between each wicket, but when the ninth wicket fell the scores were level.

For his first innings of the season, David Lewis crept out nervously into the highly charged atmosphere, knowing he had to survive the over or score one run. No doubt he was offered copious advice from

182

the other batsman, but in the end opted for a bold strike to win the day.

After lengthy re-setting of the field, the crucial ball was bowled. Lewis, making an ungainly cross-batted swipe, got a top edge, sending the ball thirty feet in the air for a comfortable catch half way down the pitch. The supercharged atmosphere was fully revealed in the mayhem that ensued.

By prior agreement, the batsmen set off, heads down, to dash to the other end. Cover, mid-wicket and the bowler, were each determined to make the catch their own, converging on the same spot all shouting 'Mine!' An almighty pile-up and scrum ensued, with the five players spreadeagled or knocked yards off course, the ball falling virtually untouched in the middle.

The bowler was the first to his senses and with the wicketkeeper crouched over stumps screaming for the ball, a run-out looked certain. Seized with excitement, his brain must have switched off, because he ignored the shouts and hurled it at the unprotected bowler's wicket. He missed, and the ball raced unhindered to the boundary for four overthrows.

Peter Withers was a fine medium pace bowler, who played for St. James's in the '70's. He tells of an incident in a match for Reading against Teddington in '57, which, in a visual sense, remains the funniest I've come across. It also goes back to the days when a bowler showed concern for a batsman hit by a ball, and highlights a hazard of this nearly forgotten courtesy.

A middle order batsmen had been in for some time, scratching around picking up the odd single, from the tight bowling of Withers and his colleague. Eventually in frustration, he summed up courage to go for the hook, succeeding only in getting a top edge.

The ball flew up onto his cheekbone, then lobbed gently into the waiting hands of second slip. As he completed the shot, legs straddled across the wicket, he fell from the force of the blow, impaling himself painfully on the off stump.

If all this wasn't grief enough, he'd gasped with shock when hit, and

The lawn/cricket ground in front of the Chateau de la Fresne
KOB

his false teeth had popped out to land near the crease. Withers, alarmed by the carnage he'd initiated, followed through and rushed on down the pitch to offer assistance. Unfortunately, in so doing, he trod on and broke the false teeth.

The tragic picture evolves, of the poor fellow limping painfully towards the pavilion, bat under arm, remnants of false teeth in one hand, the other clutched to staunch the flow of blood from his cheek! It wouldn't have been the done thing to laugh openly, but how could anyone have kept a straight face?

———⊰❈⊱———

When Ian Boyd-Pain took over as 'mine host' of the 'Battle of Trafalgar' in Brighton, he gained the perfect platform to regale all and sundry with the spectacular feats of his cricket career. The hot air reached the ears of a female customer, married to a Frenchman who'd played some cricket while a student in England, and eager to play the game.

Out of the blue an invitation and challenge arrived, to play a match against the town of Falaise in Normandy. Honour bound to accept, B-P didn't realise the French had developed quite an interest in cricket, so assumed it would be a 20 over slog they'd win blindfold.

The fixture was confirmed for the August Bank holiday Sunday of '89, and the team, cobbled together from anyone vaguely associated with the pub, decided to make it a boozy weekend over the water. On the Friday evening they assembled at the pub, and piled loads of tinnies plus cricket kit into the boots of three cars. Not knowing what to expect at the other end, they also took a decent jacket, shirt and trousers, in case they ran into anything formal.

Thus equipped they set off for the Dover ferry, found a boarding house in Boulogne, and spent most of Saturday on the French equivalent of a pub crawl. Heavily hung-over they faced a 150 mile journey to Falaise, birthplace of William the Conqueror, on the Sunday morning.

It was a stinking hot day, with the lads in festive mood and dressed little better than beach bums, when they set off for the estimated three hour drive. Due to meet their opposition at mid-day, having motored at speed down the wrong road for forty miles, they were over an hour late when they pulled into the Falaise town square.

As they fell out of the cars, they were pounced on by three agitated Frenchmen, who explained they'd have to hurry immediately to meet the reception party, with no time to change clothing. They stumbled through a crowd milling around the bandstand, where a dozen musicians in red jackets and gold braid, were pom-pomming away with 'Colonel Bogie'.

They assumed some important event was taking place, and asked their hosts what it was all about. The reply, that they were on parade to welcome an English cricket team, caused jaws to sag in disbelief. When they further learnt that lunch in the Town Hall was next on the agenda, fags were rapidly extinguished, and pathetic attempts made to comb hair with fingers and straighten non-existent ties.

It was sweltering heat, over 90 degrees, and the welcoming party had been standing in the sun on the Town Hall steps for over an hour. The Mayor and councillors, in full ermine robes and tricorns, were sweating and visibly wilting as they awaited their guests.

After much smiling and handshaking, the bemused Englishmen were ushered into the Town Hall, to the Mayor's Parlour for cocktails. As a fleet of waitresses constantly recharged glasses, the pub team, in cut-off jeans, sweat shirts and flip-flops, mingled self-consciously with their formally attired hosts.

Next move was into the Dining Room, where 60 people sat down for a four course meal, lashings of wine, and much merriment, as our boys fought to string together a few words of O-level French. At the end, the Mayor stood up to say among other things, how honoured he was to welcome a proper English cricket team, and hoped the occasion would advance the spirit of the European Community, as well as the entente cordiale.

Reeling out of the hall, the 'Battle of Trafalgar XI' were escorted the short distance to the 'ground', at the Chateau de la Fresnaye. It was an impressive, historic, stone building with a 30 yard wide gravel apron across the front. Acres of gardens spread in all directions, with the entrance drive circling the lawn in front, about 50 yards across by 70 deep.

This immaculately maintained lawn provided a ready made, if small, playing area, and as the grass outside the drive sloped upwards, with a curtain of pine trees at the top, a natural amphitheatre was formed.

As the motorcade swept round the drive to park at the back of the Chateau, the Englishmen were surprised to see so much activity going on, but when they walked round the front to take in the full scene, they could hardly believe what they saw.

Dozens of cars were parked in the side roads, with more arriving every minute, while some spectators had enjoyed a picnic lunch on the slopes prior to the event. A television truck from the local TV station was parked just outside the circle, with cables strewn around, plus a public address system with speakers on poles in the four corners of the arena.

It should be said not all the crowd had become cricket lovers overnight; there was also a Calvados wine tasting festival taking place in front of the Chateau. On repeated questioning of B-P, as to the numbers present, he started at 400 and had moved up to 800 by the last time of asking. Whatever the truth, it was certainly by a factor of 10, a bigger crowd than he'd ever entertained before.

The next shock was when the lads strolled out to take a look at the pitch. A strip had been cut in the lush lawn with a cylinder mower, but they'd only made one cut, about 24 inches wide! The bowlers in the side could be seen to sober up on the spot, as they thought about the task ahead.

Tactfully, nothing was said about that, the teams changed in the Chateau and Falaise won the toss and batted. As the Battle XI took the field another problem came to light; there were no stumps! The hosts hadn't got any, and assumed – not unreasonably – that no English cricket team would go anywhere unless equipped with the full paraphernalia of the game. In fact, the Battle XI could only rustle up a few balls, in various states of disrepair, and nothing much else.

Desperate measures were called for, so one of the Frenchmen dashed to his nearby home to find something suitable. He grabbed a saw, ran into his back garden and pulled up several of his precious runner bean poles. Apparently his wife was watching all this from the kitchen, and could only stare in open mouthed amazement, as he frantically hacked them about.

Racing back to the Chateau, the stumps were put in and a bail taped across, enabling the players to take the field. Excitement mounted as the TV reporter swung into action, providing a running commentary for the live spectators as well as the home audience; his style being more Peter O'Sullevan than John Arlott.

Prompted by a English cricket lover holidaying in Falaise, he reported the action with detailed explanations to the fascinated audience, his only problem coming when B-P went on to bowl. Either there isn't, or he didn't know, a suitable translation for spinner, so he called him the 'demon flicker', a term which much appealed to B-P.

It was clear some of the Falaise team had played before; in fact several had picked up the basics of the game while students in England. But the Battle XI were more or less in control of events, and taking wickets regularly, wrapped up the Falaise innings for 93 just before tea.

It had been an enjoyable session, a minor hiccup occurring when B-P broke a bean pole stump with an off-break – something he attributed to vicious spin rather than speed. And it was noted that the commentator got more excited over the fielding than the strokeplay, with the crowd energetically applauding even the simplest stop and return.

A long trestle table had been set up for tea at the foot of the Chateau steps. Laden with all the usual goodies, it was clear someone had done their homework on the traditions of the English cricket tea. There were piles of dainty cucumber sandwiches without crusts, and after discreet searching it transpired there were only cucumber sandwiches without crusts. But there was a splendid assortment of fancy cakes, and the cups of tea were of the finest Earl Grey blend.

The Battle XI went out to bat and, though they had to think about it, knocked off the runs fairly easily with three down. But they tried hard to entertain the crowd, delighting them with some big sixes far over boundary and spectators. It had all been great fun, and certainly something new and different for the majority of those present.

After the match the players gathered at the steps where a cup was presented to the English side, necessitating a few words of thanks from skipper B-P. Surprisingly, he was not entirely unprepared having brought a new bat for this possibility, and uttered out a couple of sentences in schoolboy French. This went down well, but he gave up when trying to describe his gift, calling it 'le cricket bat'.

The hospitality continued with the players invited to the homes of the Falaise team, to freshen up prior to an evening meal at Au Grande Dequesne, the smartest restaurant in town. Now comfortably on Christian name terms, they settled down for a multi-course meal, interrupted by many hospitable toasts, as the teams ate and drunk the night away. The Battle XI then stayed overnight with their hosts, before parting company on the Monday morning to drive home.

For all concerned it was an unforgettable weekend, and hardly the quick beer match they'd expected. And it only occurred to B-P too late; the French may have thought it provocative, or gloating even, that the English team called themselves, 'The Battle of Trafalgar XI'.

———❧———

The Sussex Martlets are one of the 'jazz hat' club sides, at one time a stepping stone for talented youngsters into the County side. With players drawn from the leading Sussex clubs, another distinction was playing their midweek home matches at Arundel Castle, accepted by many critics as England's finest club ground.

With that background, Dick Packham tells a lovely story which, to me, perfectly illustrates the best laid-back, 'friendly' club cricket tradition. It took place in '78, after several of the leading players had previously decided the fixture list needed moving 'up market'. They'd arranged a fixture against Emeriti, the well known London area nomadic Club.

When the players arrived for an 11.30 start, it was a perfect, warm, cloudless day, and with the pitch prepared to county standards, the prospect of first strike was a mouth watering one. Sure enough, Martlets won the toss and batted, but Rowdy Yates, Dick Packham and John Davis, all failed to take their chances, and were soon back in the pavilion. But Andy Meads and Robbie Barker got well established, and at the one o'clock lunch interval Martlets were about 125 for 3.

When play got under way after lunch, the three disappointed batsmen were joined by bowlers Tony Reilly and Sandy Ross, plus skipper Martin Bodenham, to form a card school. Also, to help while away the afternoon a bottle of port was ordered, so as the batsmen made hay outside, the players became locked in an intense card game, and the bottle of port turned into a six bottle round.

Having got through five, heavy hints were dropped to skipper Bodenham that it was his turn. He was about to do the necessary, when he suddenly remembered there was also a cricket match going on, and rushed outside to see the state of play.

Frantically looking round for the scoreboard, he mouthed a strongish expletive and wheeled his arms energetically to signal the declaration. Unusually, it was not only in the middle of an over, but the bowler was running in for the next ball.

It was then nearly four o'clock, and both batsmen had been anxiously looking for the signal for some time. Martlets had scored 327 for 3, with Meads 142 not out and Barker well on the way to his century. Bodenham struggled hard to dream up a credible excuse for the belated declaration, while Andy Meads was grateful for one of the longest knocks of his career.

Emeriti had been left just over two hours playing time to get the runs, and I'm told the atmosphere between the sides was, 'somewhat strained'. I also understand the fixture was not renewed.

CHAPTER 13

INDELIBLE MEMORIES

Anyone looking back over a long cricket career, is likely to do so with sentiment and nostalgia for the grounds, games and players they've been involved with over the years. In this last chapter I thought I'd indulge myself even more, by jotting down some of my performances which, for one reason or another, remain indelible memories.

Its always amazed me how professional cricketers can not only recall details of their batting or bowling throughout their careers, but often the state of the pitch and weather as well. Maybe it's something to do with the tension and adrenalin being that much higher.

In my case, and I suspect with most club cricketers, I remember nothing of hundreds of trips to the wicket, and just the haziest outline of a dozen or so. Maybe they've stuck in mind because I was nearer a 'star' on these occasions, rather than my usual 'domestic' role.

Like every schoolboy, I dreamt of being the 'Roy of the Rovers' character, or playing the 'Boy Wonder' role on the cricket field. I also assumed that in my club career, I'd get plenty of chances to enact these fantasies over the years. In fact, there was just one match which I could claim qualified me for hero worship.

It was for the NALGO XI in a mid-week evening match, 20 overs a side, at Wish Road Recreation Ground in Hove. The pitch was soft, wet and slow, as there'd been plenty of rain in previous days. But memorably, the outfield grass was four or five inches long, as the gang mower had broken down, so the Council hadn't cut it for three weeks.

The Opposition batted first and scored 85 and in reply NALGO were about half way there when I went to the wicket. Batting was not easy with the ball skidding through low, and if you struck it off the square it slowed rapidly, making fours a rarity. We concentrated on 'tip and run' to keep the scoreboard moving, but still wanted six from the last over.

With tension mounting and some audacious, scampered singles we got to the last ball, with me facing, still needing three to win. The field was already spread round the boundary, only cover and mid-wicket being closer. Hitting the ball past them to the outfield would only bring two at most, so I had to hit a four, or preferably, a six.

There was no lengthy field adjustments, as everyone was already in place, so the bowler ran in for the last ball without much fuss. He was a steady medium pacer who'd not caused much trouble, but, in the conditions, was not easy to score off. As a pessimist even then, I was resigned to the probability I wouldn't be able to hit a six, as that simply wasn't my kind of shot.

Heart pounding, I faced up with no clear idea of what I was going to do, but was surprised and delighted to receive a juicy half-volley just outside off stump. It was the perfect ball for me, and I lashed into it with every ounce of strength, sending it skimming past cover's left hand at speed. Nevertheless, it was still going almost straight to the man in front of square on the boundary, who carefully kneeled down for the stop. But luck intervened, or more precisely, the fielder behind square intervened.

He raced round to intercept, skidded across the path of the ball trying to slow down, and ruined it completely for his colleague. From the tangled limbs and desperate grabs, the ball somehow escaped and flopped over the rope for four.

Absolutely elated, I'm sure I must've tipped my head back, lengthened my stride, and with a flourish, tucked bat under arm as I set off for the pavilion. Applause from my colleagues was unrestrained as I neared the boundary, but I also became aware of a commotion behind me.

The two fielders I mentioned had exchanged views heatedly, but nothing like the furious row with all the four-lettered words, which developed between the bowler and his skipper. Apparently the bowler had not realised, and reckoned he'd not been told, that it was the last over. He thought there was still one to come, and made no special effort with the actual last ball, resigned to us getting them anyway.

———◇◈◇———

It's ironic that the longest certainly, and one of the most important, innings I played was for the Brighton Council XI in Stanmer Park in August '62. A mid-week match, it was a bright, warm day, perfect for cricket, and with no rain in the previous weeks, the pitch was hard and relatively fast.

The opposition were St. Francis Hospital Staff from Haywards Heath, and it was soon clear most of them were regular club cricketers. They arrived keyed up for a competitive game, discussing tactics and agonising over the batting order. They seemed to know nothing about the Alderman, so I assumed it must have been a new fixture.

When I looked round our changing room I was appalled; it appeared to be the weakest Council XI I'd played in, though there were several new, unknown faces. St. Francis batted first and by luck, two of the Alderman's last minute fill-ins were useful bowlers, and he had the good sense to keep them on most of the afternoon. There was no one else capable of bowling even remotely near the stumps, so I thought we did well to contain them to 180 for six at tea.

The batting order I remember clearly; I was to open with a chap called 'Bonny', a friend of the Alderman and occasional player. Number three was Tim McCoy, the former Brighton and Hove Albion footballer and, as it turned out, a very useful cricketer. The Alderman was at four on merit, and after that there appeared to be nobody capable of holding the bat up straight.

Walking out to open that day, I felt weighed down with responsibility, certain that if I got out quickly, the game would only last another hour at most. Determined to do our best, and concentrating on defence like mad, we survived the opening spells from two sharpish seamers. As confidence grew and nerves subsided, I played a few shots, though Bonny didn't seem willing or able to get the ball off the square. He finally succombed for 18 when we'd put on 54.

Tim McCoy settled in easily, and the runs began to flow as he played some powerful straight drives. We enjoyed a fruitful partnership of around 70 till he was out for 36.

As the Alderman shuffled out, I reflected that he was just old enough to be my grandfather, and this surely, was the beginning of the end. Though I only expected him to last a few balls, I still felt obliged to try and shield him from the bowling, adding further to my worries.

In fact the St. Francis bowlers were having trouble controlling their swing, a lot of deliveries curving down the leg side, feeding the

Alderman's favourite shot, the shovel to leg. Remarkably, receiving no straight balls, we built a mini-partnership for twenty minutes or so, though running between the wickets was pretty nerve wracking, as we turned easy twos into hairy singles.

When St. Francis at last got rid of the Alderman, I'd scored about 70 and we were within sight of hanging on for a draw. Also, with only half an hour to go, they would have to dismiss each batsman quickly or they'd run out of time. I scored a few more but was aware of growing mental fatigue; I was in uncharted waters as I'd never batted that long before.

I'd reached 85 and was past caring, only interested in putting my feet up with a pint. I lashed out at a ball outside off stump, and was relieved to hear a loud click before a louder appeal. With relief I turned to walk off, but saw the 'keeper standing, head in gloves, ball between feet.

I batted on in a trance almost, as wickets fell every three or four minutes, losing track of score and time. A draw was most likely, as we started the last over with two wickets left, and I summoned up concentration to bat right through.

Due to face the last ball, play was held up when a shout came from our scorer that I was on 95. St. Francis had still been playing it hard, hoping for the remaining wickets, but with 18 still needed a draw was certain.

With everyone relaxed, the bowler indicated he was going to toss up a friendly one for me to hit a six. To be fair, he did precisely that, bowling a slow half volley just outside off stump. All I had to do was plonk one leg down the pitch and swing the bat straight through the line. I did that but I hadn't the strength to strike it hard enough, it bounced once before hitting the sightscreen.

There was applause all round, as I dragged myself back to the boundary, an exhausted hero. Sunk in a deck chair, I was unbuckling my pads when I was aware of the Alderman in front of me:

'Well done Dick; just the innings we needed!'

As he'd always called me 'Redbourn!' before, it was a prized accolade; I'd joined the inner circle of Brighton Council XI cricket.

I've mentioned Derek Pickering several times previously, and one of our many batting partnerships perfectly illustrates the essential difference between the 'star' and the 'domestic'. Friends since teenagers, Derek was the only person to play for St. James's throughout the whole of my 30 year period with the Club.

He played for England Schools, Sussex 2nd XI and other top club sides, and was a devastating off-spinner for a few years before he suddenly 'lost it' when he was 20. After that Derek concentrated on batting, and has scored thousands of runs over the years, initially as an opener, then dropping down the order. Batting at six or seven in the '80's, he became a versatile team player in League matches, defending, accumulating, attacking, or slogging, as the situation demanded.

The match concerned was at Goring on a bright, blustery day with the pitch firm but skiddy on top. We were batting first and I'd been given a chance up the order at three. In a couple of overs the first wicket fell and I walked out, nervously, to join Derek.

Unusually, both Goring's opening bowlers were medium paced left arm over and were pitching a touch short, on or outside off stump. The first three balls were enough to convince me I'd have to defend like mad just to survive, let alone score runs. Each delivery lifted, seamed, or swerved to some degree and, angled across the body, I found it devilishly difficult to decide which to play at or leave.

I could see Derek was not finding it much easier at the other end, but, with increasing frequency, he was able to get on top of the ball and deflect, or angle it through the gully area. As I hung on grimly, riding every piece of luck, we built a useful partnership lasting nearly an hour till I was castled.

As I walked back, proud of my efforts in a hostile situation, I felt I'd made a worthwhile, gritty contribution to my team's performance. We'd put on 55 for the second wicket, I'd scored 6.

———⇒✿✿✿⇐———

During the '70's I was working for a manufacturer in Crowborough called Fair-Air, with a staff of about 70. It was a pleasant summer, so someone had the bright idea of challenging another firm of similar size, Servomex, to a 20 overs-a-side evening cricket match. Date and venue were fixed and it was solemnly agreed there'd be no ringers, only full-time employees of each Company being eligible.

No self-respecting club cricketer enjoys this sort of shindig, it's usually a travesty of a game, and a waste of time for a regular player. I was the only practising cricketer in Fair-Air, and in fact, the only person who'd played a game since their schooldays. As everyone was taking the thing seriously, I knew I'd be expected to perform miracles and win the match single-handedly if necessary.

Nearer the day, we heard on the grapevine that Servomex had got a 'star' performer lined up, so we asked Terry Grimes of Crowborough C.C. to play, on the grounds that his wife worked for our firm. There was a keen buzz of anticipation, serious practice held in the car park every lunch break, and the odd bread roll tossed up in the canteen.

Although I was hoping for rain, it turned out a bright, but windy evening as we left work on the dot for the ground. It was up on the hill at Jarvis Brook and, as it was used regularly for club cricket, had most of the essential facilities. We'd borrowed some stumps and basic kit and everything was ready as we assembled in the changing room. Terry and I had brought our normal kit, but as I glanced round the room there was not a white plimsoll, or even a near white shirt, in sight.

I didn't protest too much when appointed skipper, at least I knew roughly what was supposed to happen. Servomex batted first and, self conscious in my proper kit, I led my men out. I picked someone to bowl and, as no-one knew fielding positions, told the rest to spread themselves around about 30 yards from the wicket.

My heart sunk when I saw the Servomex openers on their way out. One, mid twenties, tall, blond, athletic, looked like a 'megastar', with all the kit including thigh pad, chest and arm protectors.

The 'megastar' disdainfully left the first ball, about a yard down the leg side, but confirmed his status on the fourth. Short, but somewhere near the target, he rocked onto the back foot and, with a lazy, straight pick-up, lifted the ball over the sightscreen.

We were powerless to do anything about the torrent of runs, until over-confidence struck on the second ball of the third over, 33 already on the board. The 'megastar' went for a full bloodied cover drive, the ball popped and he got an outside edge, sending it steepling high into the sky over cover. With the height, the blustery wind and spin, it was a horrendously difficult catch at any level of the game.

Panic struck when I realised I was under it, and the other fielders were all expecting me to do the necessary. As an experienced 'domestic' cricketer, there was normally only one course of action in this situation; to shout a firm, commanding, 'Yours!', and back-pedal rapidly away from the landing area. Yet I could see there was no-one nearby remotely interested, let alone capable, of holding it.

What's more, I was supposed to be a proper cricketer, and would've suffered total loss of face if I'd chickened out. And crucially, it could've been the last chance of preventing the 'megastar' becoming the first player to score a double century in a 20 overs match.

I just had to go for the catch. It was swirling around so much I was leaping rather than shuffling about, to stay under it. With heart pounding, I lunged forward at the last instant and grabbed it, rolling over in sheer relief. I was miffed that none of my team-mates applauded, or offered congratulations; presumably they thought it was all routine stuff for a cricketer.

With the 'megastar' gone the standard levelled out, the bowlers couldn't pitch near the wicket, and the batsmen couldn't make contact if they did. Servomex got to 83 in 20 overs with most of their side getting a knock. The percentage of wides and no-balls must've been high, but all our chaps got a bowl so everyone was happy.

Excitement was high in the changing room, all anxiously awaiting the order, assuming I'd elect to open with Terry Grimes and myself. A trifle patronisingly I announced:

'Look; this game is for your fun. Terry and I'll take ten and jack. I suggest you draw out of a hat for the first nine'.

That was well received, duly organised, and the second half got under way.

One of the Servomex bowlers looked as if he'd played a bit in the distant past, but otherwise it was evenly balanced. Singles were scampered, a wicket fell every couple of overs, and with extras we were up with the clock for a while.

With no limit on overs per bowler, the Servomex 'star' began to put it all together, it was too much for our batting and runs dried up as wickets fell. Suddenly I was donning pads rapidly and on my way to the crease at 42 for eight. Within an over it was 42 for nine with Terry at the other end. We held a mid-wicket conference, if only to agree the situation was serious with only seven overs left.

We employed all our accumulated experience, pinching singles without taking chances, while coping with a highly variable attack. The 'star' bowler was not dangerous but had to be respected, but from the other end, sorting out the succession of beamers, daisy cutters, wides and full tosses, needed great care.

We got there at the start of the last over, and walked off to wild cheering and a hero's welcome. In all senses I felt I needed a cold shower, but there weren't any of course.

———◈◈◈———

I didn't play much in the '89 season, but got the call one August Saturday, to turn out for the 2nd XI that afternoon. We were one short for a League match against Rye on our ground, so, without much enthusiasm, I got down there just in time for the two o'clock start.

Ashamedly unfit at 16 stone and completely out of practice, I was very much 'going through the motions', at that stage of my 'career'. Yet not only did it turn out to be a superb game, a fine example of the best type of competitive League match, but it also marked a belated personal milestone.

Looking back over the years, on those few occasions I put together a decent innings it was usually against weak opposition and someone else would have scored them anyway. Or if I defended like mad in the middle order, it might have staved off defeat for a draw. Ridiculous it may seem, having played all those matches, but this one would have to be the likeliest candidate for where I may have changed the course of the game, from defeat to victory.

To get the facts right, I managed to rescue the scorebook before it was thrown into someone's attic. The salient points of the game, with my tenuous claim to heroism, are as follows.

St. James's batted first on the matting wicket, and scored 204 for 5 declared after 49 overs. This took about half of the five hours play for the match, and tea was taken between innings. Rye started batting and lost wickets at 6, 13 and 56 when Roy Wheeler joined Ian Addy at the crease. Both men were essentially First XI top order batsmen, having a run out in the 2nd team after injury.

After a careful start, they got into their stride and the run rate climbed alarmingly. They found the easy pace and predictability of the artificial wicket just to their liking, and when the score reached three figures were totally in command of events. We tried switching our bowlers, but they treated all-comers with the same disdain.

While all this was happening I'd been skulking around on the boundary, at fine leg or long-off, trying to keep out of the way of the ball. When forced to join the fray, I used my soccer skills from an earlier age to cut off any fours I could reach, and bowled the ball back in a gentle parabola as swiftly as muscles would allow.

By the time the score reached 125, Addy and Wheeler were turning the contest into a rout; they'd put on 69 in 12 overs with the run rate still increasing. With the simple target of scoring 80 in 10 minutes plus 20 overs, another quarter of an hour of this battering and the game would've been won and lost.

I was at long-off on the boundary when Addy, on 76, launched into a ball from young James Shillaker with a full-bloodied, low, straight drive, which I picked up about the top of its flight path.

Someone cleverer than me, has since calculated there was one and a quarter seconds from that instant, till the ball reached me at a shade over 60 miles an hour. As my adrenalin shot up, such is the speed of the human brain the sequence of my panicky thoughts in that time went something like:

'Good God; that ball's coming my way!'

'There's no way I'm going to catch that.'

'If I do it'll hurt like hell.'

'I'll have to fake a near miss – but that's not easy.'

'Cripes it's going to hurt.'

'I don't need this in my state of health.'

'We need this wicket desperately.'

'There's no alternative; I'll have to go for it.'

I dropped onto one knee, knowing there was no way of 'giving' with the ball, forwards, backwards or sideways. It hit my hands at waist level, just to the left of my body and, by locking elbow onto hip, I managed to catch and stop it in the space of a foot or so.

Immediately aware of intense pain, I looked down to see blood spurting under pressure, from a cut on my index finger. I was shocked, frightened even, as I'd never seen this before, and fleetingly imagined if it went on for long I might 'empty'.

I went off for repairs and a swig of something, while the game continued in different mood. The new batsman was very much 2nd XI middle order and Wheeler felt obliged to shield him and tone down the attacking shots for a while.

With the tail exposed, we took wickets at 141, 156, 176, 184 and 188, when the last man came in. They scrambled some singles, but Wheeler clearly had little faith in his partner and, with three overs left, tried to finish it with a big hit. He was bowled for 62 and Rye were all out for 199.

I watched all this going on with great pride, and in the bar later had to stop myself claiming I'd personally won the match single-handed. My 'injured' finger healed leaving a small, permanent scar, a prized momento of the occasion.

Just one technical point; as an experienced 'domestic' cricketer, faking a dropped catch has been a basic part of my armoury, but in this instance difficult to achieve convincingly. It was a dull, overcast day so, 'sun in the eyes' was not a viable excuse. There was no wind and the ball was driven hard and low, so I couldn't suggest it was swerving about.

As it was coming straight towards me, I couldn't move sideways pretending to misjudge the line of flight. Again, if I'd run forward implying miscalculation of the length, it would've still been catchable around head level. And if I'd have gone backwards, I'd have allowed the ball to bounce in front of me, or tripped over the boundary rope, looking a complete idiot.

I suppose I could've flapped a hand at it as it went passed, but that would've been obvious cowardice and I still had some pride. Going for the catch was probably the only viable option!

———◆◇◆———

I played my last match in August '92, when a pal of mine Derek Barnard, roped me in to make up the numbers for Crowborough 3rd XI, in a Sunday game at Walstead School near Lindfield. The team were mainly Colts, and, on a warm weekend at an attractive ground I'd never played on before, I thought it might be interesting to see the lads in action.

We fielded first and I was quite content to patrol the boundary, with splendid views across the countryside, as Lindfield 3rd scored 185 all out by tea. There was plenty of athletic fielding from the youngsters, though the bowling could have done with a bit more 'line and length'.

After tea in the changing room, I was about to look for the nearest deck chair, when Derek courteously asked me to open the batting. With a laugh, I turned the offer down with:

'No thank you Derek, I'm well past it; I'll go in at number eleven'.

Immediately a stern, older voice from a dark corner of the room replied:

'Oh no you won't. I'm number eleven. I've been going in at number eleven for Crowborough for twenty years or more.'

Hastily I settled for number ten and, having trodden on toes, I'd learnt something new; I'd never realised there could be serious competition for the last place in the batting order.

I got my deck chair and watched with amazement, a precocious thirteen year old score 90 before he ran out of strength. Then we started losing wickets regularly and, reluctantly, I had to pad up. When the eighth fell, I had to go in with 48 needed to win from four overs and one ball.

As I hadn't batted much in three years, I knew it was only a question of the first straight ball, so I was surprised to see the 18 year old non-striker hurrying across the square to meet me. Surely he wasn't going to warn me it was swinging away, or keeping low, or something? But as soon as he reached me, while struggling to get my gloves on, he anxiously asked:

'Whadaya reckon then?'

A long shadow at the end of an innings

Being well out of touch, my mind raced around trying to fathom out what he was talking about. Impatiently, and clearly expecting pearls of wisdom from such a veteran campaigner, he repeated the question, 'whadaya reckon then?' As I still fought to get on his wavelength, he couldn't contain himself any longer:

'Well I reckon we oughta go for 'em.'

I burst into laughter, which I tried to stiffle, – one shouldn't discourage the young – then nodded furiously in agreement. It was a prime example of the exuberant optimism of youth, and the cynical pessimism of experience.

I believe I lasted four balls and the resident number eleven, five. That was that, but it had been a pleasant day out, with plenty of enthusiasm from the next generation.

In serious vein, looking back over my playing days, the fundamental things I miss now are no different to those of any club player: the release from winter hibernation, the warmth of a sunny spring day, the smell of freshly mown grass, the sound of willow on leather, and so on. Then for me, there were those very rare occasions when everything was perfect: the weather, the ground, the pitch, the game in hand, and the excitement of racing between the wickets, chasing quick runs, constantly wiping sweat from brow with soaked shirtsleeve.

All that, however much missed, might be described as the obvious, physical attractions of the game. But to me, above these was the spirited, exhilarating repartee we enjoyed as we exploited the humorous potential of the 'domestic' cricketer. With years of cricketing failures and mishaps stored in the collective memory, the changing room resembled an intellectual bear garden, as we fought to outwit each other with ever more subtle and cutting jibes.

I also much enjoyed the relaxed sessions in the pavilion bar, or local pub, after a game in a mid-Sussex village, when we would update gossip, and discuss highlights of the match with the opposition. That seemed to me to be delightfully unhurried, sociable and civilised.

My generation is perhaps the last to be captivated by the deeds and glamour of the greats of the post war cricket boom. We tried to emulate the stars, without talent and technique, until we accepted our lowly place at the grassroots. By then addicted to the game, we carried on making our own fun and friends, and now, treasure the precious, indelible memories.

THE DOMESTIC GLOSSARY

Originally drawn up for 'The Domestic Cricketer', this glossary gives terms associated with 'stars' and 'domestics'.

(adv) - adverb.   (col) - colloquiallism.
(abb) - abbreviation.   (n) - noun.
(a.d.) - alternative definition.   (v) - verb.
(ch) - chapter.

Bails!! (n)	An expletive for use in mixed company
Bazooka attack (col)	A series of high altitude deliveries to test the batsman's long range vision
Beamer (n)	A swift full-bunger, aimed to decapitate
Bent (adv)	To lean heavily towards one side
Blob (n)	A duck
Blonger (n)	A blob, a duck (see blob)
Bouncer (n)	A fast short pitched ball occasionally delivered by a berserk domestic bowler (a.d. A kindly affable disco attendant)
Boundary (n)	That point in the outfield beyond which one cannot proceed without clearing tools, or mechanical cutting equipment
Boundary marker (n)	A piece of old rag, nailed to a stick, previously licked with white emulsion
Box (n)	A receptacle for personal effects
Buzz (n)	A fast, flat return to the stumps
Caress (v)	To slide the leather erotically across the greensward
Castle (v)	To knock over the woodwork, to bowl comprehensively
Chinaman (n)	A velly clever ball
Coerce (v)	To chastise, whip or smack, with the willow
Cow (n)	An ugly agricultural shot, lacking any aesthetic merit

Cream (v)	To plunder any loose or indifferent bowling
Crease (v)	To double up in hysterical mirth
Daisy Cutter (n)	A shooter or grubber; a fatal ball to a swinging domestic
Domestic (n)	An esoteric term for a player who does not expect to influence the course of events in a match
Donkey drop (col)	A domestic bowler's cunningly disguised slower ball
Drop anchor (col)	Stonewalling, blocking, boring, crease occupation
Duck (n)	A blob, blonger; failure to exercise the scorers
Family affair (col)	Father umpire, son bowler
Fend (v)	Strenuous exercise of the martial arts with the bat
Finger happy (adv)	An umpire prone to frequent and instantaneous use of the index digit
Full-bunger (col)	A high full toss; potentially lethal to domestic batsmen
'Ger on wiv it!' (col)	An impatient, impassioned plea to the batsman to elevate the scoring rate
'Gi'e it tap lud' (col – northern orig)	Freely translated as an exhortation to the batsman to commence a virulent assault on the bowling
'Give it some stick!' (col)	To cane the bowling with unabashed brutality
'Give it the charge!' (col – military orig)	To thunder down the track in a frontal assault
'Give it the ol' – heave-ho!' (col)	A joyous entertaining mixture of heaves and ya-hoos
'Go deep!' (v)	A vague instruction to a fielder, to ruminate in the rough
Google (v)	Verbalisation of the googly. (For full definition, see more learned works)
Grass (v)	To drop a catch (a.d. an informant, a soft drug)

Grope (n,v)	Basic defensive shot of domestic batsman – played well forward, off balance, with head up and bat away from pad (a.d. a furtive manual exploration)
Hammer (v)	To strike the ball with explosive, primeval force
'Hari-kari job' (col)	The frenetic and suicidal pursuit of runs, for the good of the side
Heave (n,v)	A mechanically inefficient shot; high energy input for little discernible output
Hoik (v)	To ladle the ball in ungainly fashion
Hole-out (col)	To be caught short
Hook (n)	A rusty nail occasionally found on the dressing room wall
In-ducker (n)	A ball which swings in late (not negotiable by a domestic batsman)
Jock (n)	A type of guardhouse: a structure to restrain the privates (a.d. someone from north of Watford)
Jug-shot (n)	An involuntary, run scoring stroke by a batsman nearing 50
Kitty (n)	A collective purchasing system, whereby a third of a pint of lukewarm bitter is obtained for £2
Knock (n)	A star plays an innings; a domestic has a knock
Lunge (v)	To grope desperately, as or after, the ball passes the bat
Maiden (n)	Rarely seen nowadays in club cricket
'Middle from where 'e bowls' (col)	A request for a guard to be given from the bowler's usual delivery position
'Nought for plenty'	Typical domestic bowling analysis
'One for the off'	A contrived friendly first ball to enable a batsman to 'open his account'
Outfield (n)	That part of the ground where grass can only be cut with a scythe
Pea-roller (n)	A very short delivery which maintains continuous contact with the pitch surface

Pearler (n)	A deceptively quick ball which ducks in late, pitches, whips back across and lifts viciously
Ping (v)	To despatch the ball with flippant and contemptuous indifference
Prod (n)	A stabbing forward joust
Pull (n)	Necessary forearm movement to replenish a pint
Punch (n)	A shot struck with piston like action of the lower forearm
'Push it about' (col)	A innings of indolent and facile economy
'Put down a dolly' (col)	To drop a simple catch. (a.d. to cease manhandling an attractive young lady)
Rabbit (n)	A virgin performer, undefiled by talent, technique or experience
Rogue buzz (n)	A wild mis-directed throw, wreaking havoc and carnage amongst the close field
Scorer (n)	A domestic's wife, capable of putting two and two together
Shocker (n)	A star batsman's description of an l.b.w. decision
Shooter (n)	A domestic batsman's explanation of an l.b.w. decision
Shout (n)	A discreet invitation to the umpire to consider the adjacency
Sight-screen (n)	A piece of torn grey canvas, designed to flap behind the bowler's arm and distract the batsman
Skipper' round (col)	An obsolescence, a thing of the past
Slash (v)	To despatch the ball with a vicious, late Karate chop (n.b. perfected by Jim E Riddle, Lancashire)
Slog (n)	A innings with high proportion of heaves, cows, tonks and ya-hoos
Smear (n)	A ferocious, head up, cross-batted heave to leg
Smear (v)	To play an innings of violent, but effective, inelegance

Snick (n,v)	The fortuitous result of a grope
Snorter (n)	A vicious, venomous delivery, unplayable by any batsman
Squirt (n)	A belated shot, squeezing the ball away from the stumps (a.d. young son of a gentleman)
Star (n)	A player possessed of talent and confidence, who expects to influence events in a match
Steer (v)	To deflect the ball with geometric precision
Swing (n)	Unwitting and uncontrollable aerial movement by a domestic bowler
Swoop (v)	A one handed, hawkish lunge at the ball by a star fielder, demonstrating athleticism, aggression and other noble qualities
'Take apart' (col)	To disembowel the bowling with clinical precision
'There or thereabouts' (col)	A succession of accurate deliveries by a star bowler, virtually eliminating scoring strokes
Thrash (v)	To humiliate and desecrate the bowling
Ton (n)	A star's practical intent, a domestic's illusive dream
Waft (n)	A nebulous air-shot, avoiding contact by wide margins of time and space
'Well left!' (col)	A derogatorary compliment to a batsman after an unsuccessful grope (see Beecheno Ch. 6)
Ya-hoo (n)	A naive, exhuberant swing, refreshingly free from technical inhibitions
Yorker (n)	A ball which pitches under a ya-hoo
'Yours!' (col)	The correct call by a domestic fielder, in the vicinity of a difficult, high catch